Visit www.**BeetleReich**.com

BEETLE REICH

Beetle Reich

J. D. OKORO

Illustrated by Sebastián Valencia

Published by J.D. Okoro

ISBN: 978-0-9935286-0-6

MAP of ENTOM

Redanta Colonia

Rumyny
Boulder

Lilypad

Spruce
Vine

Lotus Flower

Roost

Pen

Fernland

Stoneland
Flatland
Leafland

Meadow

Churchyard

Mulberry

Barge Evergreen

Ducknest

Garden

Reedland

Aridland

Froot

Malt

Grayn

Barley-Rye

Gravel Tweed
Limestone
Sandbank

Toh

Farmland

Rock

Pond

Verge

Elder

Maple

Orchard

Beet

Chestnut

7

DRAMATIS PERSONAE
The Fang Brigade

Vermen Dungroll
Leader of the Fang Brigade

Pestilan Pox
Head of the Siafu

Poyson Mandible
Head of Propaganda

Hednit Grubb
Chief of the Waerozan

DRAMATIS PERSONAE
The Allies

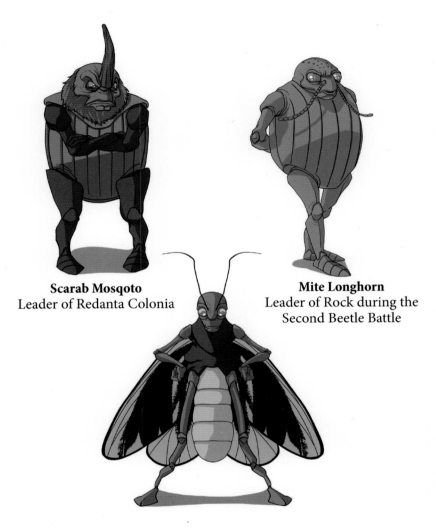

Scarab Mosqoto
Leader of Redanta Colonia

Mite Longhorn
Leader of Rock during the
Second Beetle Battle

Salix Birdwing
Leader of Orchard

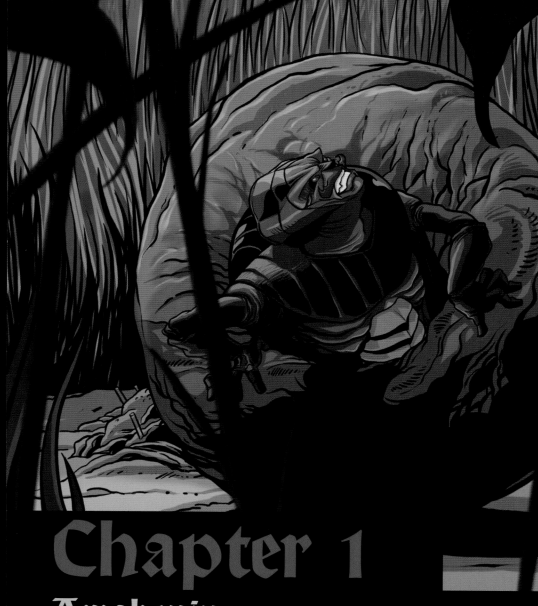

Chapter 1
Awakening

When heaven burned and queens did roar and empire spilled black blood,
Vermen Dungroll heaved free from his excremental mud.
A sphere of stench and grass it was, dead hay, no myrrh or manger.
This demon born for war would see glory, hellfire and danger.

There were with him unsavoury beasts including Pestilan Pox,
The devil's coach-horse beetle as scheming as a fox.
With them his clan known as the Fang Brigade quickly sought to
Revive their nation's fortunes, this they thought was overdue.
Their nation was called Reedland and had just lost a great war
Known as the Beetle Battle, its surrender left it floored.
It was forced to shrink in size and stopped from having certain things
Including a grand fighting force, no acids and no stings.

Reedland is on planet Entom,
Where our tale unfolds;
Where actions become legend
And great fables will be told.
Entom is a place you can see
Every single day,
Down there where the ants scamper
And slugs slither away.

Reedland

The bloated Hednit Grubb was a prized recruit of the Fangs:
"Airborne hero of the great Beetle Battle", he sang.
Then, he flew alongside the Red Mayfly, winged ace.
Soon he would head swarm attacks over Entom's airspace.
Hednit's appetite for power matched his lust for food.
He was vain, somewhat pompous, self-important, often rude.
His body, yellow-white and podgy, rippled as he went.
His shiny orange face held eyes full of hostile intent.

Also in this clan was arrogant Rumen Underwing;
A blowfly, friend of Dungroll and third in the Fang ranking.
His thick and darkened antennae and often deathly looks
Distinguished him from all of the other Fang Brigade crooks.

His colleague, Pox, had low morals yet held his head quite high;
This was small-minded, wide-mouthed and with two cold glassy eyes.
Officious and malicious and ambitious he was indeed,
Well organised to carry out Dungroll's heinous needs.
Pox's attire was solemn with a subtle oily sheen
Which matched his personality, shadowy and mean.
His poise was of a scorpion, his strut was of a goose.
It would not be long before his crazed ideas would be let loose.
He hated ladybirds and those not from Reedland for sure:
"I will hunt and then destroy them all, every last one", he swore.

But Dungroll was the yeast with which the Fang Brigade did rise.
Enchanted by his promises, the nation sympathised.
He blamed other kingdoms for Reedland's shattered state
And used every opportunity to broadcast his cold hate.
He accused the Orchard, Sandbank, Rock, red ants and ladybirds.
Dungroll's message soared and Reedland's heart was stirred.

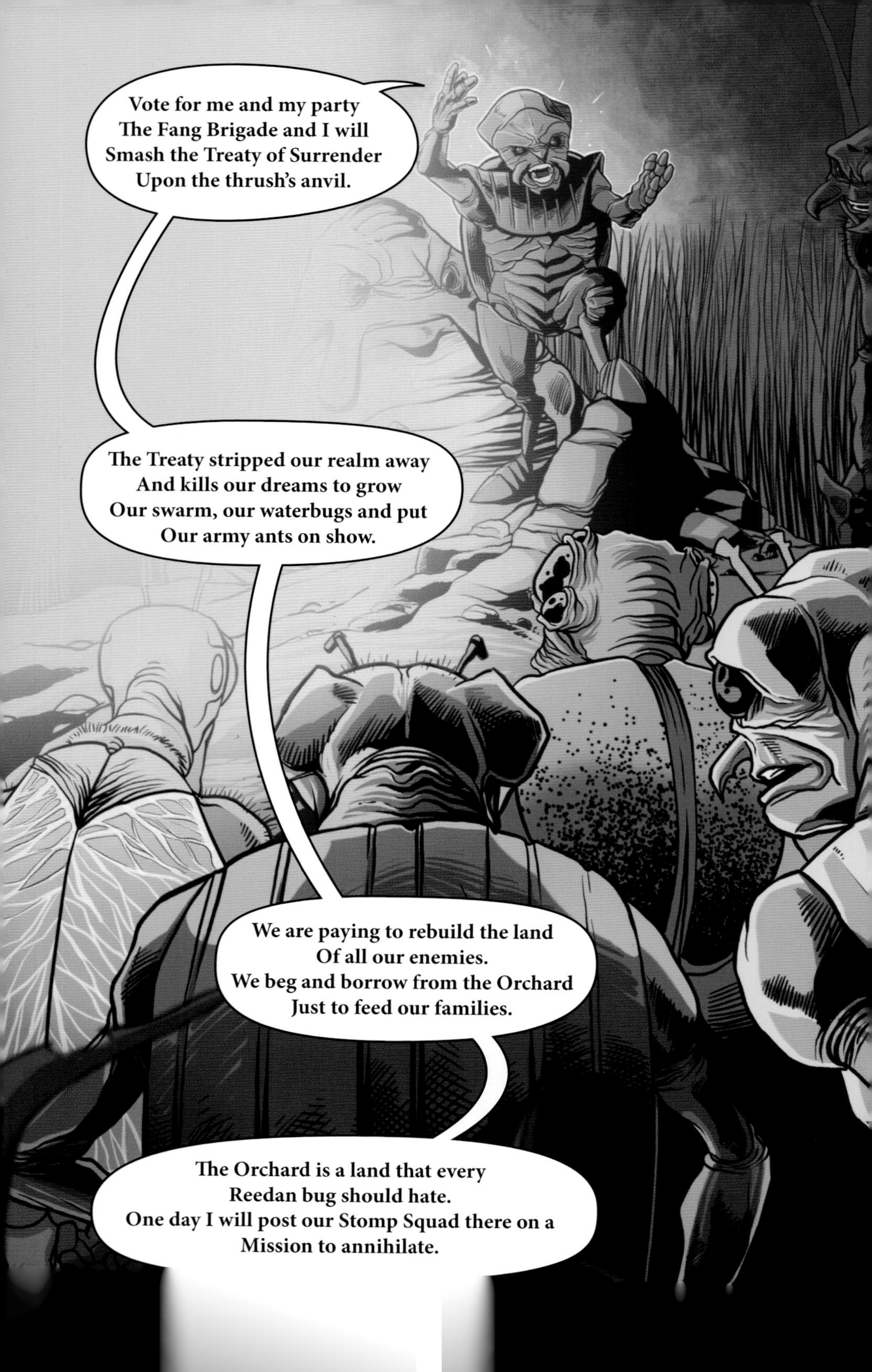
Vote for me and my party The Fang Brigade and I will Smash the Treaty of Surrender Upon the thrush's anvil.
The Treaty stripped our realm away And kills our dreams to grow Our swarm, our waterbugs and put Our army ants on show.
We are paying to rebuild the land Of all our enemies. We beg and borrow from the Orchard Just to feed our families.
The Orchard is a land that every Reedan bug should hate. One day I will post our Stomp Squad there on a Mission to annihilate.

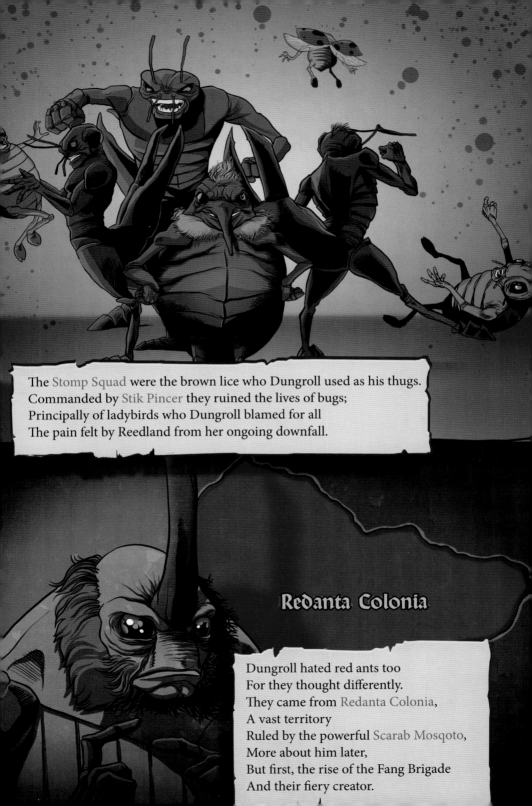

The Stomp Squad were the brown lice who Dungroll used as his thugs.
Commanded by Stik Pincer they ruined the lives of bugs;
Principally of ladybirds who Dungroll blamed for all
The pain felt by Reedland from her ongoing downfall.

Redanta Colonia

Dungroll hated red ants too
For they thought differently.
They came from Redanta Colonia,
A vast territory
Ruled by the powerful Scarab Mosqoto,
More about him later,
But first, the rise of the Fang Brigade
And their fiery creator.

Chapter 2
The Rise of the Fang Brigade

Bee Hall was an empty hive that leaders travelled to.
A place to chatter and announce what their clans aimed to do.
For Dungroll and his Stomp Squad it was time to launch a coup.
They marched to Bee Hall, stormed the chamber, wounding quite a few.

He forced the clan leaders to give their support to the Fangs
But shield bugs came and grabbed him, thwarting his revolting plan.
For his crimes he was sentenced and sent to Venus jail.
The red ants rose and the Fangs shrank without Dungroll on bail.

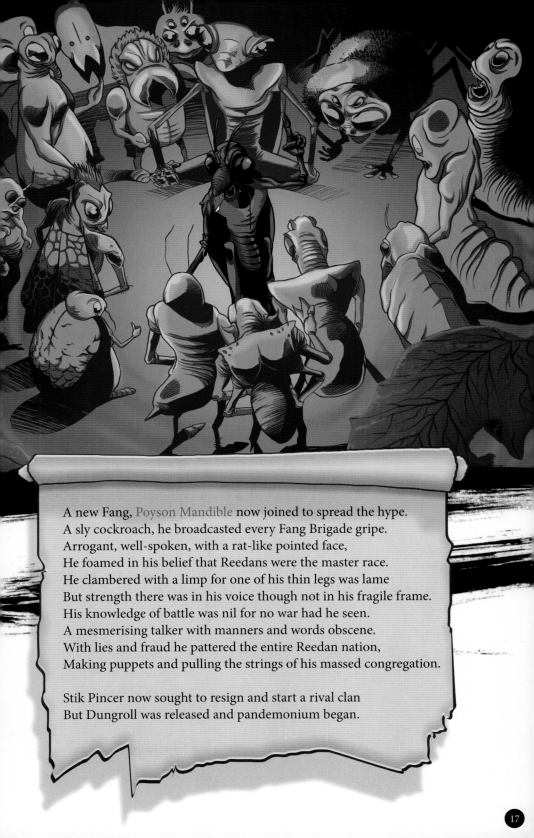

A new Fang, Poyson Mandible now joined to spread the hype.
A sly cockroach, he broadcasted every Fang Brigade gripe.
Arrogant, well-spoken, with a rat-like pointed face,
He foamed in his belief that Reedans were the master race.
He clambered with a limp for one of his thin legs was lame
But strength there was in his voice though not in his fragile frame.
His knowledge of battle was nil for no war had he seen.
A mesmerising talker with manners and words obscene.
With lies and fraud he pattered the entire Reedan nation,
Making puppets and pulling the strings of his massed congregation.

Stik Pincer now sought to resign and start a rival clan
But Dungroll was released and pandemonium began.

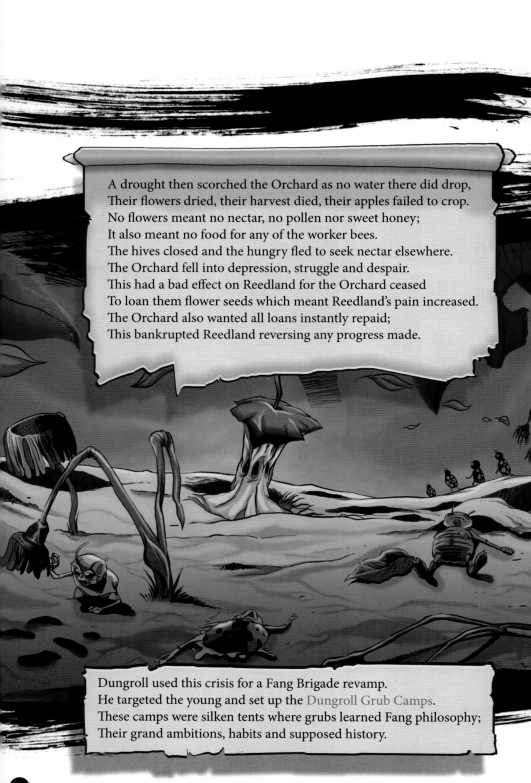

A drought then scorched the Orchard as no water there did drop,
Their flowers dried, their harvest died, their apples failed to crop.
No flowers meant no nectar, no pollen nor sweet honey;
It also meant no food for any of the worker bees.
The hives closed and the hungry fled to seek nectar elsewhere.
The Orchard fell into depression, struggle and despair.
This had a bad effect on Reedland for the Orchard ceased
To loan them flower seeds which meant Reedland's pain increased.
The Orchard also wanted all loans instantly repaid;
This bankrupted Reedland reversing any progress made.

Dungroll used this crisis for a Fang Brigade revamp.
He targeted the young and set up the Dungroll Grub Camps.
These camps were silken tents where grubs learned Fang philosophy;
Their grand ambitions, habits and supposed history.

Soon a generation rose with Fang mentality.
Dungroll was their master, non-Reedans the enemy.

Dungroll was from Aridland, he did not come from Reedland
So Poyson made him attaché to the nearby Grassland.
This was a Reedan province so it meant that he could be
A Reedan citizen and run for power finally.
He took this chance immediately to preach and to complain
To his vast audiences on his election campaign.

Yes in Beetle Battle he did
Slay some red ant beasts
And he was elected leader as his
Heroics increased;
But that septic, ancient, over-privileged,
Swollen, brainless nit
Makes Reedland melt in pigeon slop
And drown in cuckoo spit.

He is grandiose and paunchy,
By him I am deplored.
A grizzled spittlebug,
His age is an insect record!
Schooled in the old school,
A moderniser he is not.
Gruff, obnoxious, obsolete,
The bug that time forgot.

It was he who during Beetle Battle
Told Monarch to flee.
It was he who gave our land away,
Supporting the Treaty.

Dungroll spread his anthem far using every technique.
By day, grasshoppers chirped his words, by night, shrill crickets shrieked.
Ticks spread his word by foxback. The Fang emblem, termed *"clawko"*
Was etched in leaves and airborne seeds and commas flapped it low.

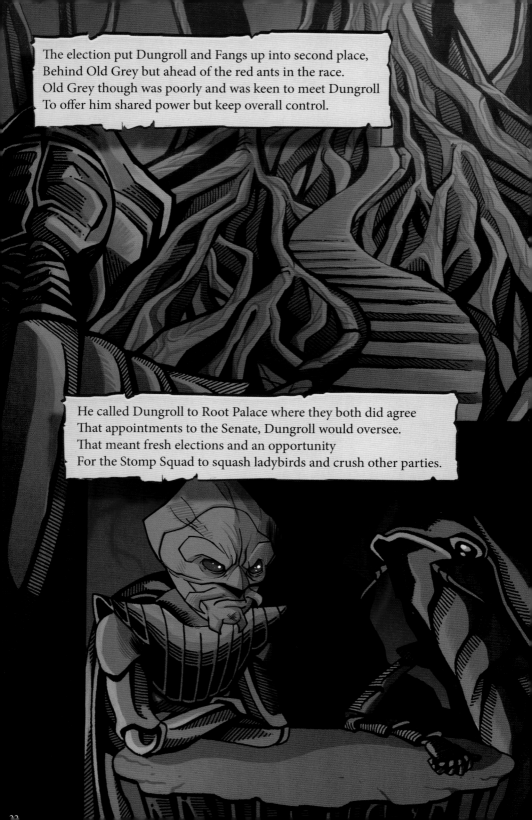

The election put Dungroll and Fangs up into second place,
Behind Old Grey but ahead of the red ants in the race.
Old Grey though was poorly and was keen to meet Dungroll
To offer him shared power but keep overall control.

He called Dungroll to Root Palace where they both did agree
That appointments to the Senate, Dungroll would oversee.
That meant fresh elections and an opportunity
For the Stomp Squad to squash ladybirds and crush other parties.

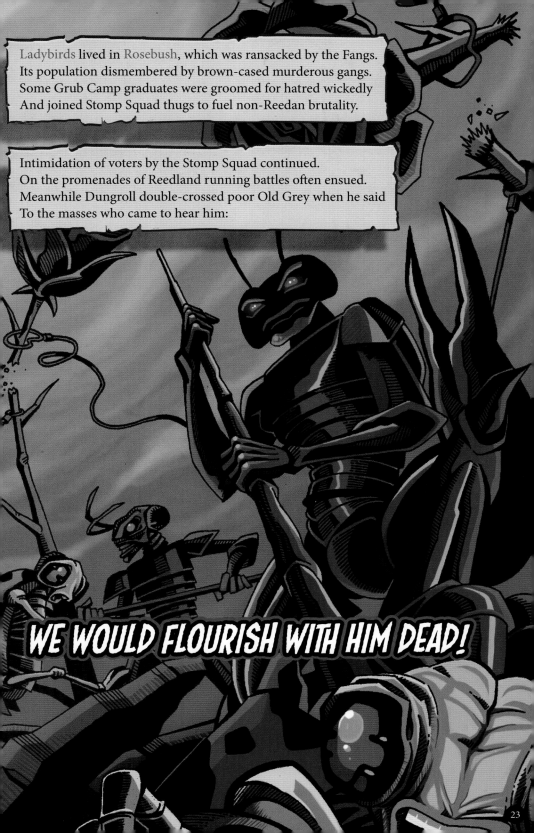

Ladybirds lived in Rosebush, which was ransacked by the Fangs.
Its population dismembered by brown-cased murderous gangs.
Some Grub Camp graduates were groomed for hatred wickedly
And joined Stomp Squad thugs to fuel non-Reedan brutality.

Intimidation of voters by the Stomp Squad continued.
On the promenades of Reedland running battles often ensued.
Meanwhile Dungroll double-crossed poor Old Grey when he said
To the masses who came to hear him:

WE WOULD FLOURISH WITH HIM DEAD!

The momentum of the Fang Brigade swept them to victory
But their share of the vote was not a two-thirds majority.
This meant that Dungroll could not be the leader on his own;
He needed to share power, the seeds of trouble had been sewn.
On hearing this damning news Dungroll flew into a rage.

"This is the worst possible outcome
For us at this stage!
Henchbugs, let's go to Root Palace
And persuade the old fool
To step aside tonight and give us
The mandate to rule!"

So Grubb, Poyson, Pox and other
Senior Fangs too
Followed the fuming Dungroll as he
Stormed out of the room.
They scuttled to Root Palace for a
Showdown with Old Grey,
Both lambasted each other,
There was much they had to say.

Old fool! It was a law that saved you,
Reedans favour me!
I demand to be the Vice-Emperor
Of this colony!

Dungroll, you risked it all and failed,
You lead a bankrupt clan
That is severed down the middle,
Your Fangs are not your fans.
Filas Fungrus for example,
Criticises you
And wonders, if he switched sides,
What he and I could do.

I will not make you Vice-Emperor
Since your ego will inflate.
Your Stomp Squad is out of control,
You spread terror and hate.
You are violently angry
With a fury felt by all.
You have a towering aura though
You yourself are not that tall.
You are utterly unstable
Of both mind and of spirit.
You will always be an outsider.
In here you will not fit.

Your plans are total fantasy,
Your delusions matched by few.
Such a poisonous orator has rarely
Been seen hitherto.
You are not even from Reedland,
You are an Arid vagabond
Who is as welcome as the plague
But we Reedans won't be conned!
Again, all I shall offer you is
To work alongside me.
Envision all the wondrous feats
We could do collectively.

By now Dungroll's mind was lost
And could not be engaged.
Instead he heated up and snarled at
Old Grey as he raged:

You prehistoric trilobite!
You parasitic bug!
You louse! You worm! You detrivore!
You yellow-bellied slug!
You can keep your paltry offer,
You must think I am a fool!
I will leave you to your madness
But I will return to rule!

And with that Dungroll skulked off with his henchbugs just behind
But Old Grey halted Filas Fungrus to toy with his mind.

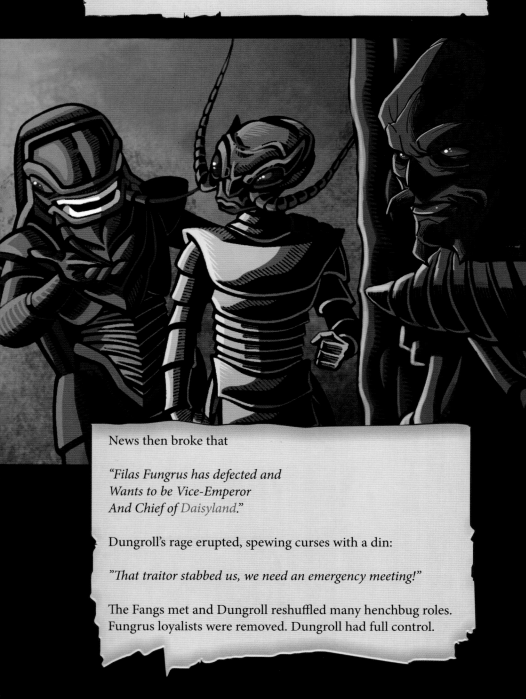

News then broke that

"Filas Fungrus has defected and
Wants to be Vice-Emperor
And Chief of Daisyland."

Dungroll's rage erupted, spewing curses with a din:

"That traitor stabbed us, we need an emergency meeting!"

The Fangs met and Dungroll reshuffled many henchbug roles.
Fungrus loyalists were removed. Dungroll had full control.

Meanwhile in the Reedan ward of Lower Daffodil
Fangs won a local election to lead a small council.
Although the win was trifling, Poyson hyped it up to be
A cataclysmic critique of government policy.
Old Grey, fretful at this loss, concocted a new plan:

"Our ministry is floundering, we will lose to the Fangs."

He invited Dungroll back and when he saw him he began:

I wish to forge a coalition
With your noble clan.
You will have infinite power,
You will be my deputy.
You will be the Vice-Emperor
Of this vibrant colony.

Dungroll pondered for a moment,
Hiding a golden smile.

Sir, I would be honoured to work with you... for a while.

That night the Fangs did revel at their meteoric rise.
The Stomp Squad illuminated by a thousand fireflies.
Countless legions of Fang members paraded through Skyberry.
Dungroll Grub Camp fellows trilled the tunes of victory.
Next day, Dungroll commanded a fresh election for Reedland.
Poyson now had every mode of media to hand.
Butterflies were used as banners, leaf-miners carved posters too,
Grasshoppers chirped the Fang message, the Stomp Squad maimed a few.

Hednit Grubb was masterminding this campaign throughout the land,
Sending Stomp Squad thugs to Quarry to take glass grit from the sand.
From the glass they redirected sun rays on to the Senate
Which caught fire as intended. Now Hednit acted irate:

The red ants have tried to kill us! We caught one causing arson!
Get Mantis the executioner. Teach these traitors a lesson!

Dungroll arrived at the burning Senate, shouting hysterically:

All red ants must be arrested! Stomp Squad show them no mercy!

He then rushed straight to Old Grey shrieking:

Sir we are under attack!
Grant me emergency powers to repel these head lice back.

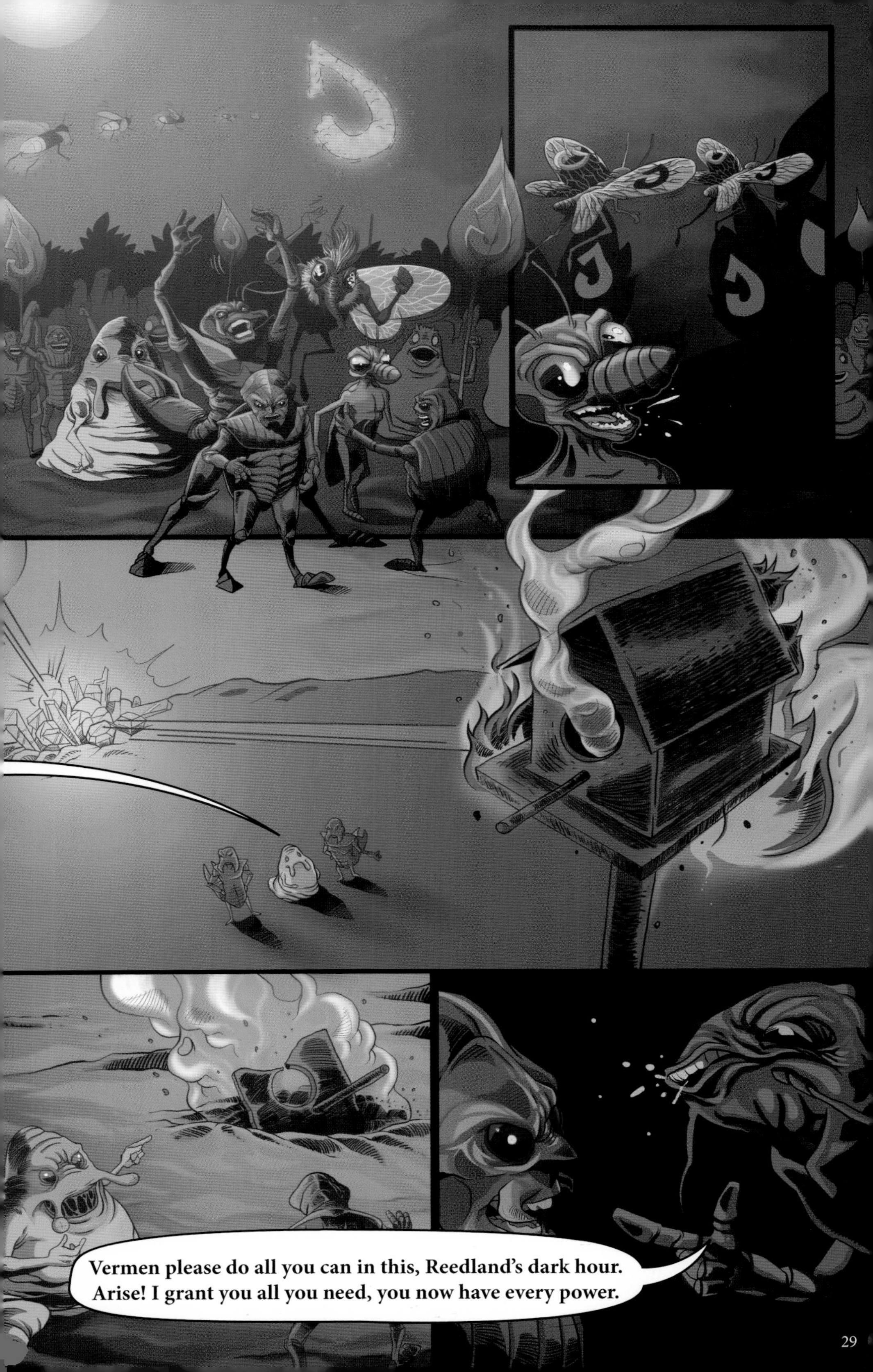

Vermen please do all you can in this, Reedland's dark hour.
Arise! I grant you all you need, you now have every power.

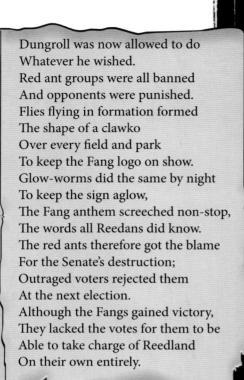

Dungroll was now allowed to do
Whatever he wished.
Red ant groups were all banned
And opponents were punished.
Flies flying in formation formed
The shape of a clawko
Over every field and park
To keep the Fang logo on show.
Glow-worms did the same by night
To keep the sign aglow,
The Fang anthem screeched non-stop,
The words all Reedans did know.
The red ants therefore got the blame
For the Senate's destruction;
Outraged voters rejected them
At the next election.
Although the Fangs gained victory,
They lacked the votes for them to be
Able to take charge of Reedland
On their own entirely.

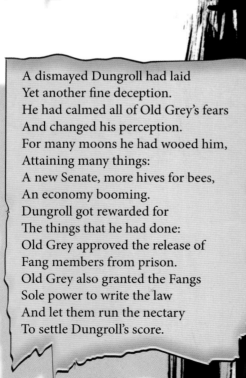

A dismayed Dungroll had laid
Yet another fine deception.
He had calmed all of Old Grey's fears
And changed his perception.
For many moons he had wooed him,
Attaining many things:
A new Senate, more hives for bees,
An economy booming.
Dungroll got rewarded for
The things that he had done:
Old Grey approved the release of
Fang members from prison.
Old Grey also granted the Fangs
Sole power to write the law
And let them run the nectary
To settle Dungroll's score.

Dungroll now had authority to be
Brutal at will.
He dissolved other clans and unleashed
The Stomp Squad to kill.
They used formic acid and their stings
Tortured and harmed,
Whilst in breach of the Treaty
The swarm was secretly rearmed.

Ladybirds trading in Rosebush
Had all their business stopped.
Their Mildew Market was shut down,
Their roses were all cropped.

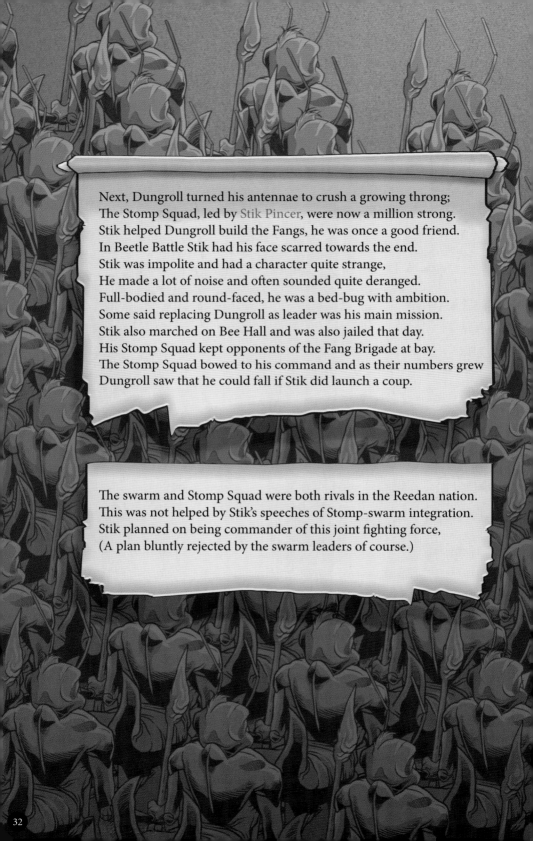

Next, Dungroll turned his antennae to crush a growing throng;
The Stomp Squad, led by Stik Pincer, were now a million strong.
Stik helped Dungroll build the Fangs, he was once a good friend.
In Beetle Battle Stik had his face scarred towards the end.
Stik was impolite and had a character quite strange,
He made a lot of noise and often sounded quite deranged.
Full-bodied and round-faced, he was a bed-bug with ambition.
Some said replacing Dungroll as leader was his main mission.
Stik also marched on Bee Hall and was also jailed that day.
His Stomp Squad kept opponents of the Fang Brigade at bay.
The Stomp Squad bowed to his command and as their numbers grew
Dungroll saw that he could fall if Stik did launch a coup.

The swarm and Stomp Squad were both rivals in the Reedan nation.
This was not helped by Stik's speeches of Stomp-swarm integration.
Stik planned on being commander of this joint fighting force,
(A plan bluntly rejected by the swarm leaders of course.)

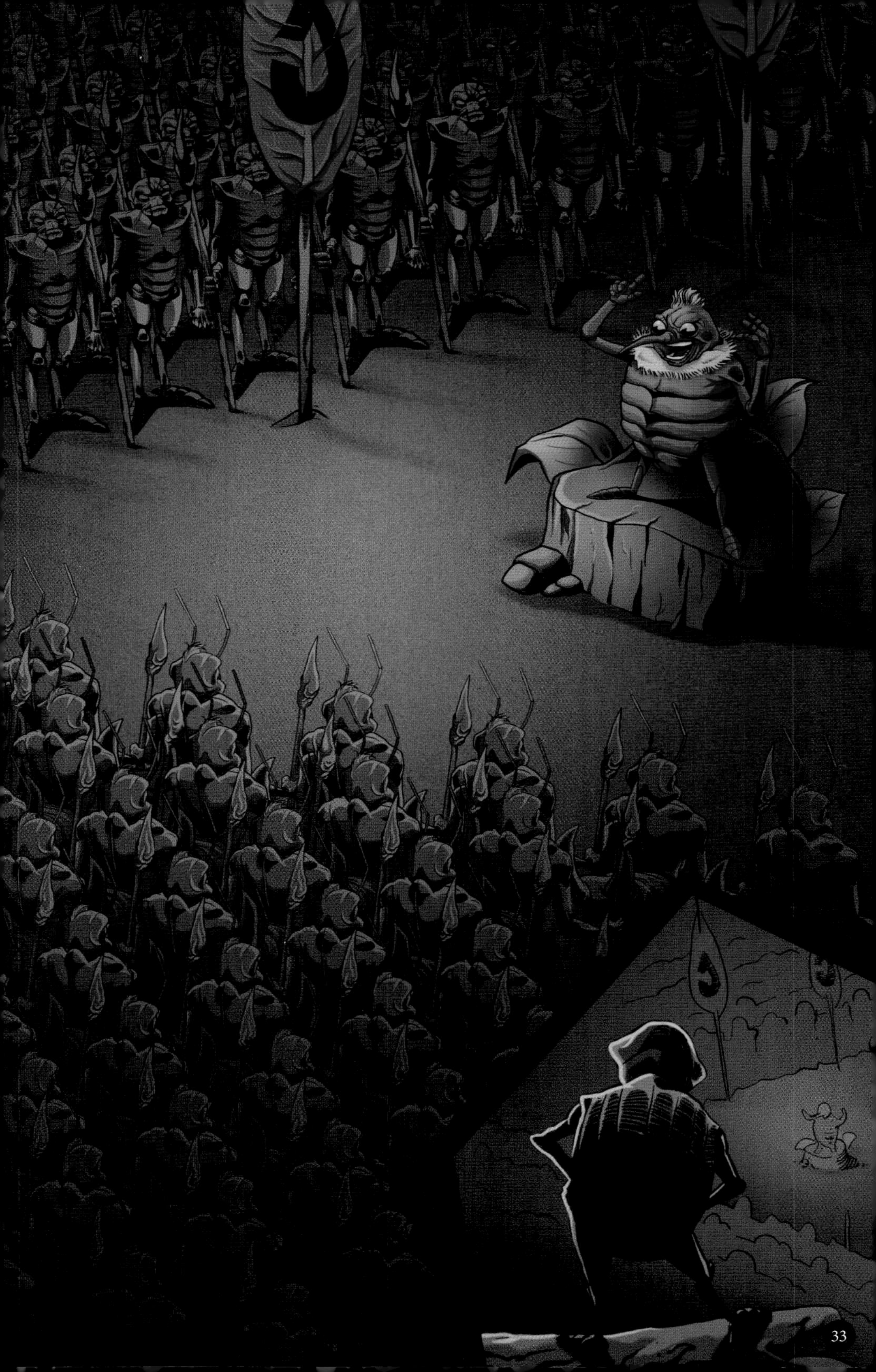

Dungroll sought to service the swarm leaders' every whim
To stop them even thinking about overthrowing him
So he had secret meetings with them to get them on his side.
He promised to regain the swarm's confidence and pride:

**You will be the only fighting force in Reedland as I said.
There is no place for the Stomp Squad. I want Stik Pincer dead!**

Outside Root Palace the next day, Dungroll put on a show
For his henchbugs, of the new horror that was set to go.

We need a new armed force
Which aims to serve and protect me.
A deadly band of warriors
To fulfil our destiny.

Pestilan Pox then stepped forward and he boasted to Dungroll:

They are ready sir, and waiting,
They are under your control.
They are the most savage soldier ants
That we have ever bred.
They were born to serve you, primed to kill
And have been selected
For their absolute Fang support
And perfect breeding too.
Sir, it gives me great pleasure to
Introduce the Siafu.

At that moment there was a loud cry replied by a roar,
Shrill notes of alarm and then a tramping not heard before.
The undergrowth exploded in a cloud of brown leaf litter.
Dust arose and grasses swayed as a battalion of critters
Darkly clad with huge jaws gaping, long legs and fiery eyes
Marched into the parade ring, much to the henchbugs' surprise.

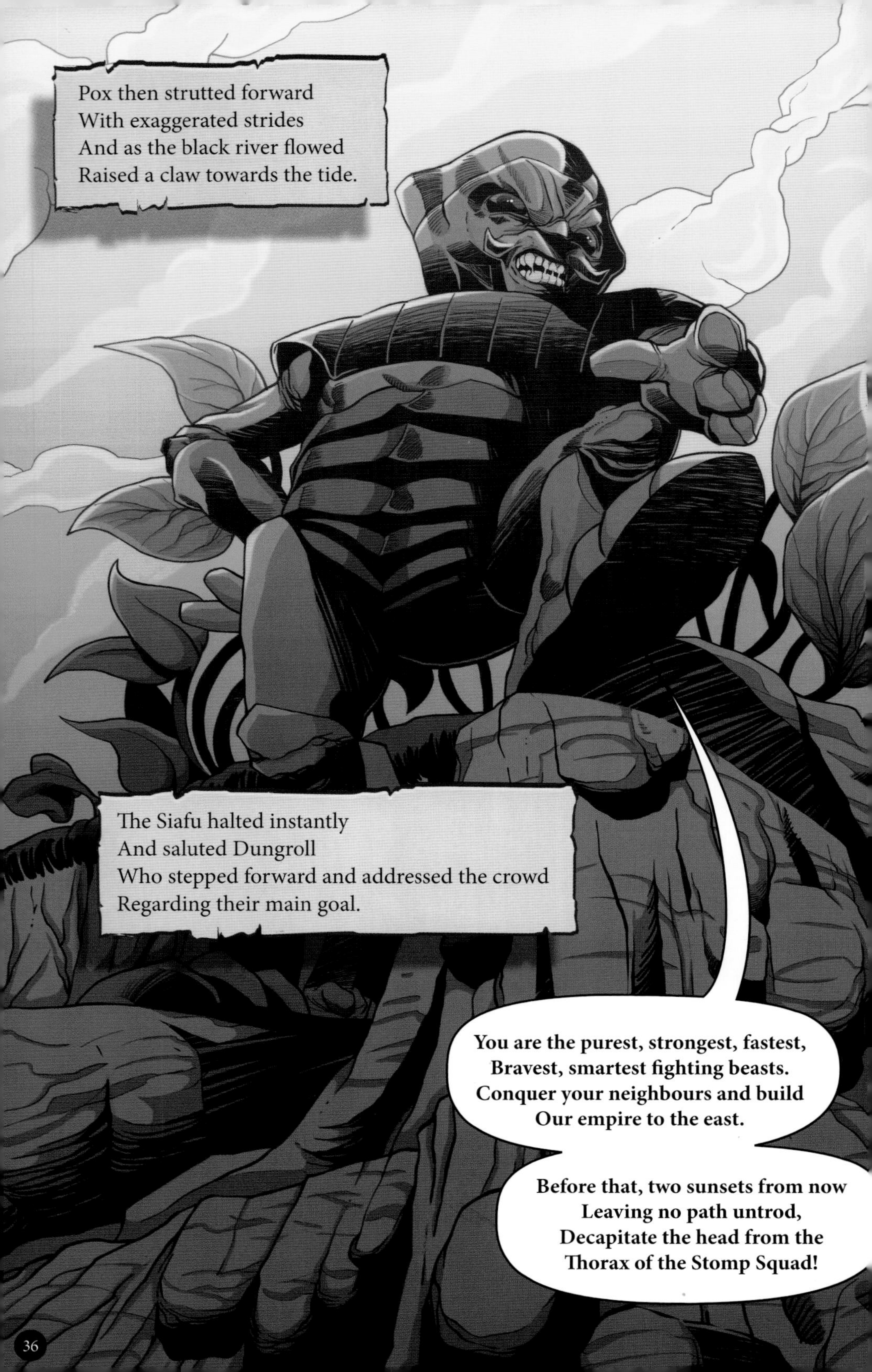
Pox then strutted forward
With exaggerated strides
And as the black river flowed
Raised a claw towards the tide.
The Siafu halted instantly
And saluted Dungroll
Who stepped forward and addressed the crowd
Regarding their main goal.
You are the purest, strongest, fastest, Bravest, smartest fighting beasts. Conquer your neighbours and build Our empire to the east.
Before that, two sunsets from now Leaving no path untrod, Decapitate the head from the Thorax of the Stomp Squad!

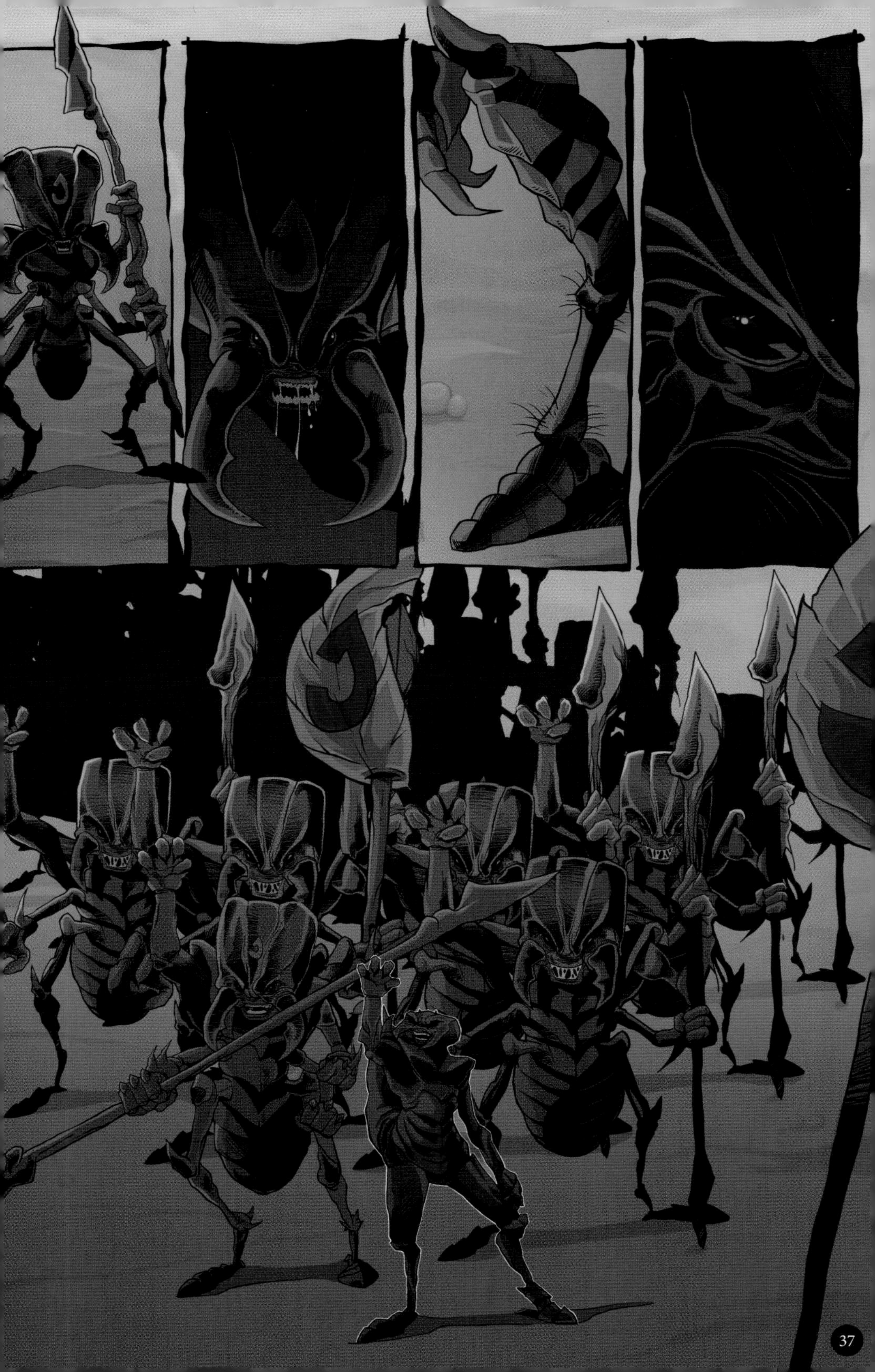

With that short message the Siafu marched off bristling.
Dungroll smiled:

Pestilan, how is
WETA progressing?

WETA, the Wrathful Extermination of Traitors Authority
Was the secret state police that Hednit had set up recently.
Hednit handed it to Pox who had managed it expertly,
Constructing termite mounds in Reedland for Fang enemies.
In these termite mounds the inmates worked until their limbs were raw
Then they were worked even harder until they breathed no more.
WETA acted upon rumour, their wicked ways were feared;
All suspects were arrested, then with no trace disappeared.

With the Siafu on his mind there was work for Pox to do
So he passed control of WETA to Grimmstone, his number two.

Pox's deputy was dastardly, younger and pleased the eye.
He was the future of the Fang Brigade, a bitter butterfly.
His wings were pale yellow and each was pricked with a small dot
Which glowed deep red as if that spot was burning very hot.

"He's spotty like a ladybird", some said. *"He must be tainted"*.
"His genes are not as pure as the image that he has painted".
Pox now replied back to Dungroll:

WETA hunts the foe

That pleases me Pestilan,
I must let Bollwax know.

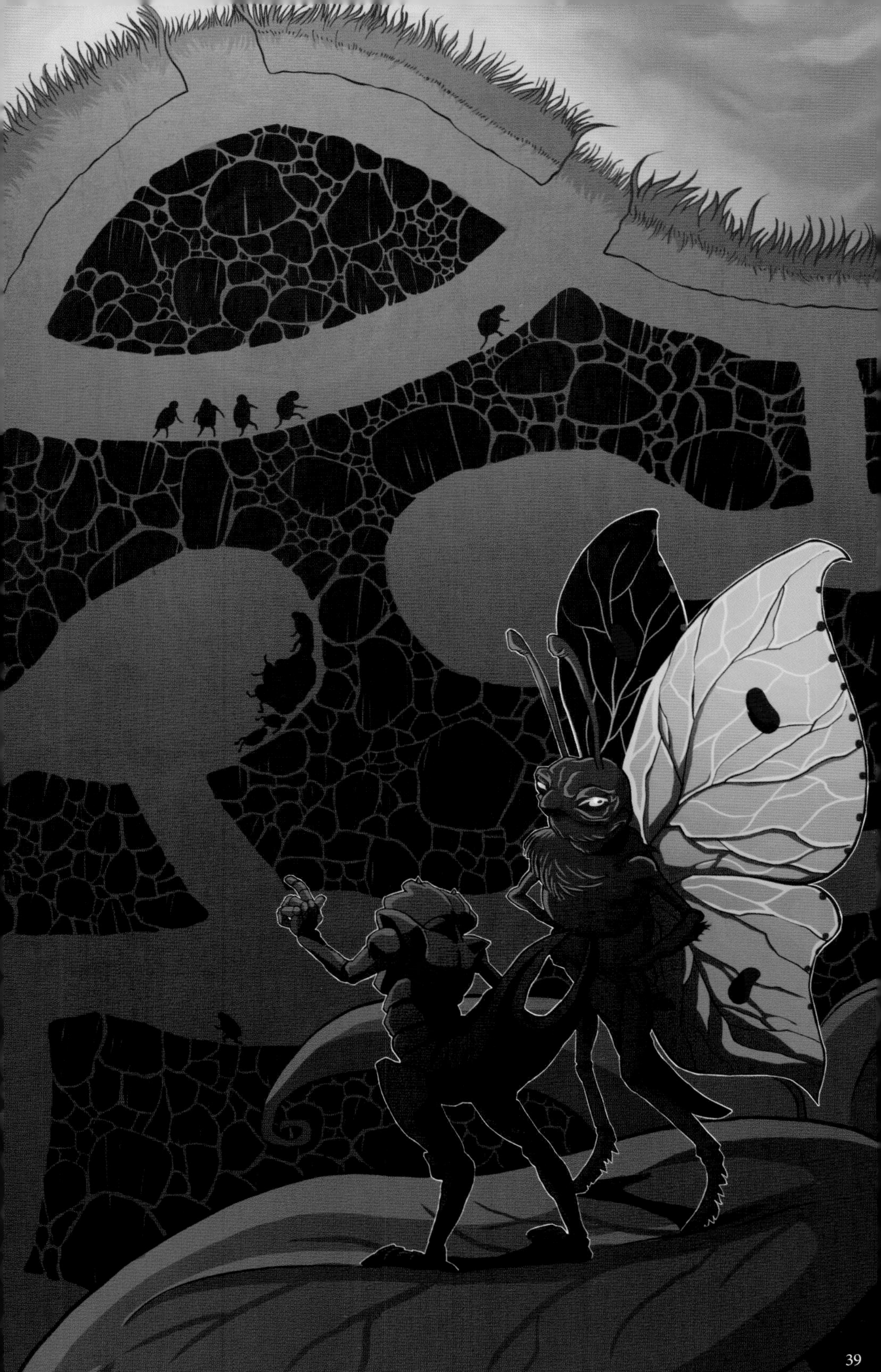

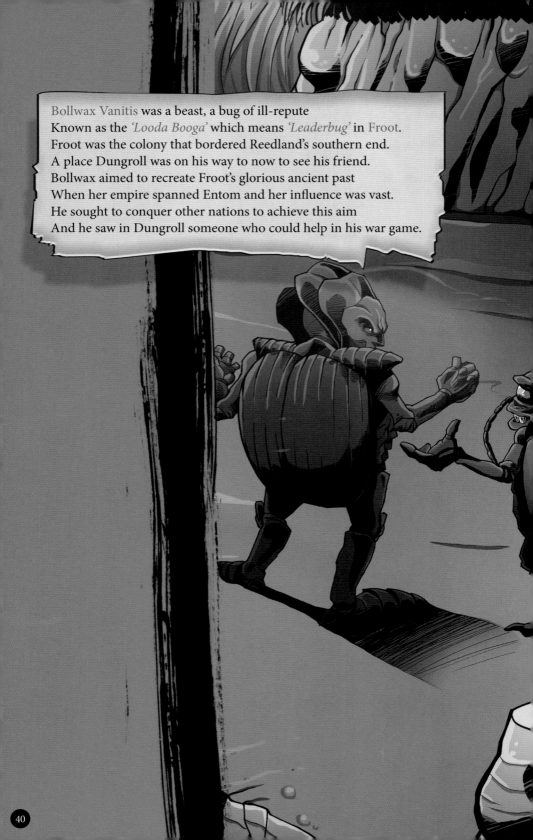

Bollwax Vanitis was a beast, a bug of ill-repute
Known as the *'Looda Booga'* which means *'Leaderbug'* in Froot.
Froot was the colony that bordered Reedland's southern end.
A place Dungroll was on his way to now to see his friend.
Bollwax aimed to recreate Froot's glorious ancient past
When her empire spanned Entom and her influence was vast.
He sought to conquer other nations to achieve this aim
And he saw in Dungroll someone who could help in his war game.

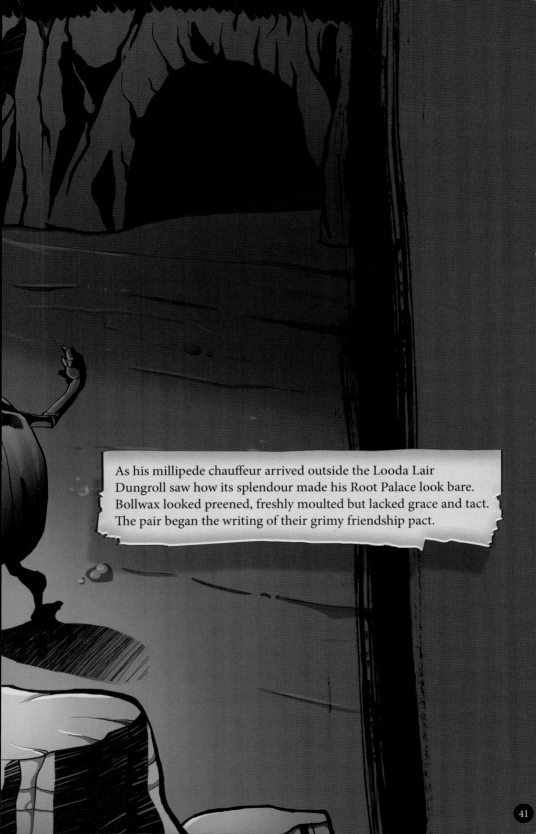

As his millipede chauffeur arrived outside the Looda Lair
Dungroll saw how its splendour made his Root Palace look bare.
Bollwax looked preened, freshly moulted but lacked grace and tact.
The pair began the writing of their grimy friendship pact.

Two suns had set since the Siafu's ominous display.
The night was nigh for the raid Dungroll ordered on that day.
Pox and Hednit had briefed them, the units were ready;
Key target located, slumbering with a Stomp squaddie.
Other victims had been pinpointed and Pox and Hednit waited
For the order from Dungroll to strike at the Stomp Squad he hated.
A hawkmoth looped and trumpeted and Pox to Hednit said:

> Look, it has the skull sign on its back,
> It is the Death's Head!

The Death's Head was the new emblem of the Siafu and
Was the sign they had been waiting for, Dungroll's strike command.

Upon this sight Siafu rampaged, hitting fast and hard.
They tore into Stik Pincer's lair, butchering his bodyguard.
They trespassed his chamber, impaled him, hoisted him up high
And proceeded to design future scars about his eye.

Dungroll stormed into the chamber and began to berate Stik.

> You conspired to overthrow me with your
> Swarm and Stomp Squad trick!
> Your Stomp Squad is being slaughtered now
> By my Siafu.
> Drink this vial of sundew juice that I have
> Kindly brought for you.

> This lets you die with honour
> For your service to the Fangs.
> There are other methods I could choose.
> Would you rather hang?

Then Dungroll left the chamber
As Stik bellowed an appeal
That was interrupted by a guard
Force-feeding Stik's last meal.

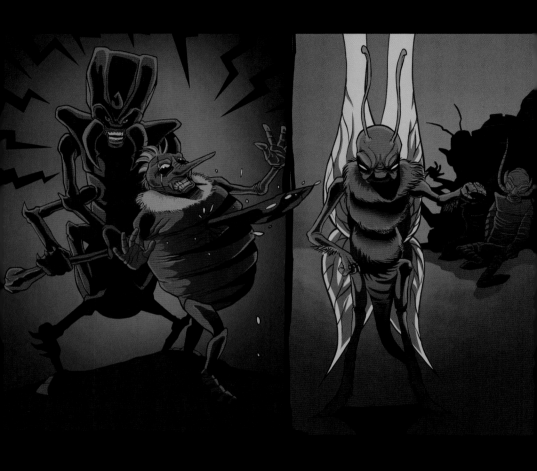

By dawn the Stomp Squad were wiped out, picked off one by one
From a bloody hit list drafted by the sinister Grimmstone.
This carnage became known as the Night of the Sharp Stings.
Even Filas Fungrus was murdered as Dungroll took care of things.

Later that season Old Grey died, it was no great surprise.
Dungroll made himself Leaderbug, objections were unwise.

Chapter 3
Expansion of the Reedan Empire

For ladybirds and red ants life was full of pain;
They were persecuted by the Fangs' murderous campaign.
Their homes in Rosebush were taken and simply gifted to
Senior members of WETA, the hydroswarm and Siafu.

Ladybirds could not farm greenfly and many were forced to flee.
Those who could got out of Reedland to escape their misery.
The Fangs continued crafting laws which did discriminate
And Poyson Mandible relished broadcasting this hate.
Screech bug and cricket leaders were summoned both night and day
To Poyson who gave them orders on what they had to say.

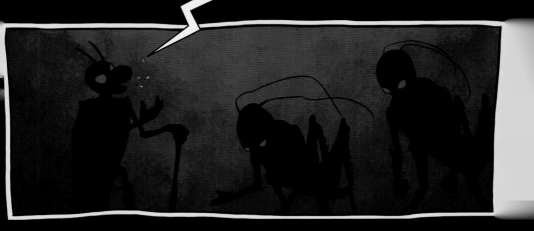

We will join Aridland to Reedland, the empire must expand!
Reedans and Arids are a family; we are both the same,
Separated by a border, we are twins in all but name.
This will not be a conflict nor a conquest, it will be
A peaceful brotherhood of equals. Life in harmony.

But Vermen how can we get
Arid's Leader to agree?

He falls tonight Poyson.
That imbecile cannot stop me.

ARIDLAND

The next day
Poyson's crickets screeched:

The Arid drone has fled!
Pursued by Arid rebels
Trying to remove his head.

This meant there was one less blockage to Dungroll's master plan
Of erasing the border between Reedland and Aridland.
This joy of the Arid drone's flight was brutishly cut short
As moths intercepted a message and gave a shock report.

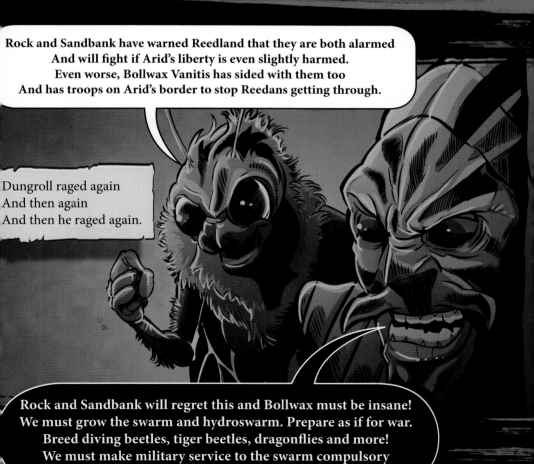

Rock and Sandbank have warned Reedland that they are both alarmed
And will fight if Arid's liberty is even slightly harmed.
Even worse, Bollwax Vanitis has sided with them too
And has troops on Arid's border to stop Reedans getting through.

Dungroll raged again
And then again
And then he raged again.

Rock and Sandbank will regret this and Bollwax must be insane!
We must grow the swarm and hydroswarm. Prepare as if for war.
Breed diving beetles, tiger beetles, dragonflies and more!
We must make military service to the swarm compulsory
So that every Reedan grub learns how to fight without mercy!

Rock's leader Spirac Nesterwing was very much concerned
At the menace of Reedland and the new land it had earned.
Dungroll preached for calm in Entom, giving a grand speech:

Do not fear us. We respect borders. The peace we shall not breach.
Arid shall remain stable, it is a place Reedland adores.
Rock we will cut our hydroswarm to a size smaller than yours.
We will retire our great stag fighters, all old wounds we shall heal.
I will send my envoy Boggum Biter to Rock to seal the deal.

Boggum Biter was a parasite, well-travelled but quite dim.
He was late to join the Fangs and other henchbugs hated him.
He was an iridescent beetle with a purple and green hue.
A hint of gold he bore with bronze and copper shimmers too.
Inelegant of manner but impeccably clad
With a bigger entourage than any queen bee ever had.
He had served in Beetle Battle with a young Reedan swarm there
And had ended many lives in that war, Entom's worst nightmare.
He had gained many honours for being very brave.
It was a shame that he still did not know how to behave.

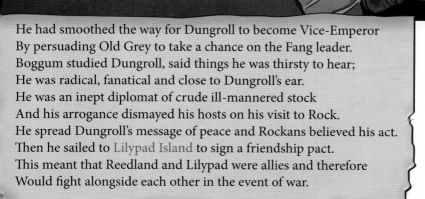

He had smoothed the way for Dungroll to become Vice-Emperor
By persuading Old Grey to take a chance on the Fang leader.
Boggum studied Dungroll, said things he was thirsty to hear;
He was radical, fanatical and close to Dungroll's ear.
He was an inept diplomat of crude ill-mannered stock
And his arrogance dismayed his hosts on his visit to Rock.
He spread Dungroll's message of peace and Rockans believed his act.
Then he sailed to Lilypad Island to sign a friendship pact.
This meant that Reedland and Lilypad were allies and therefore
Would fight alongside each other in the event of war.

Meantime the swarm and hydroswarm were racing to expand.
Dungroll chose now to reveal that he wanted to steal more land.
The land was Garden and had been part of Reedland before
But was torn away after her surrender in *that* war.
Garden was deserted, an enforced buffer between
Reedland and three neighbours: Barge, Ducknest and Evergreen.

We shall re-enter Garden with a small,
Lightly-armoured force.
No-one will try to stop us, they want
No battle of course.
But if Sandbank or Rock should oppose us
We must then retreat.
But if they don't our Treaty reversal
Shall have been complete.

Then a group of Reedan bugs re-entered Garden at nightfall.
Neither Rock nor Sandbank challenged them or resisted them at all.
Evergreen was stunned and her leader now felt all alone;
Fearing battle she proclaimed that Evergreen was a neutral zone.
Dungroll was elated, he now knew that nobody
Would stop the spread of Reedland into new territory.

Sandbank and Rock are so weak,
They are not ready to fight.
Is there really no-one out there who can
Challenge our Reedan might?

Meanwhile Bollwax Vanitis had started trouble by
Sending his Frootian swarm to storm the land of Barley-Rye.
This foray was calamitous, Froot's horde got a beating.
They came, saw, failed to conquer and were last seen retreating.

In Verge, which bordered Sandbank, a civil war now began.
It proved the perfect way to test Hednit Grubb's Waerozan.
The Waerozan was Reedland's air force which Grubb did supply
With winged beasts from tigermoth to lacewing and housefly.
Air commander Grubb used the Verge crisis to study
Secret weapons, techniques and air attack strategy.

Our spiderlings can parachute.
Our craneflies are not agile.
Our moths zig-zag when under attack.
Our earwigs are most vile.

Bollwax also sent his fliers to assist Dungroll in Verge.
Thus Reedland and Froot became allies whose tactics did merge.
Sandbank and Rock did not stop this Waerozan display.
Dungroll saw again that they would not stand in his way.

Although Reedland was thriving, Dungroll was still not satisfied.

We are cramped, our empire needs more land, we must span Entom-wide!
We have flowers and much nectar and a growing hydroswarm
With underwater bugs 'U-Bugs' much greater than the norm.
We must strike whilst our foes are weak and are not fit to attack.
Sandbank and Rock are scared of us, the Orchard will sit back!
The Orchans are happy for us to slaughter one another
And when the dust settles they plot to be the super-power.
As for Redanta Colonia they are not war-ready;
Their leader, Scarab Mosqoto has slaughtered his military.
He has killed so many generals, they are in disarray.
Let us take the Aridland now and with no delay!

By now the uproar against Dungroll's claim to Aridland
Had subsided meaning he could enter without reprimand.
He summoned Aridland's new leader to Root Palace and
Threatened to raze her realm if she opposed Reedland's demand.

Your country is unlawful, wrongful and erroneous.
Forbidden and prohibited, this charge is serious!
I indict you for high treason and charge you with theft from me.
Reedland wants Aridland, you'll die if you disagree.

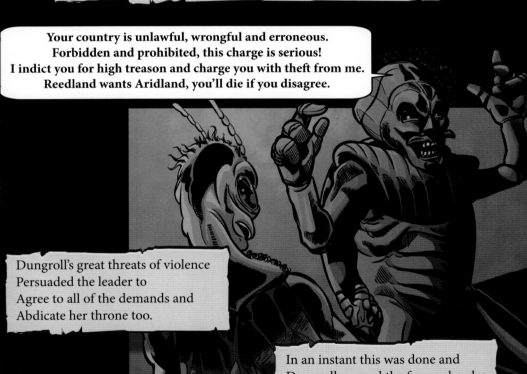

Dungroll's great threats of violence
Persuaded the leader to
Agree to all of the demands and
Abdicate her throne too.

In an instant this was done and
Dungroll crossed the former border
To see his place of birth and
Shape Aridland's new order.

So Aridland was no more, swallowed up in a bloodless coup.
A brilliant theft, a terrible crime, Dungroll's impudence grew.

They did not stop us taking Garden nor the Aridland.
We must march on and take Churchyard if we are to expand

Churchyard's ancient site was once part of Reedland
But got severed after Beetle Battle (a Treaty demand).
Her neighbour, Meadow, was also freed from Reedland's tightened grip.
Now Dungroll sought renewal of their Reedan membership.
After the Beetle Battle countless Reedans were expelled
From Churchyard to new Reedland whose population swelled.
Many died along the way as they trudged down the lane.
Now Dungroll sought revenge for this added to Reedland's pain.

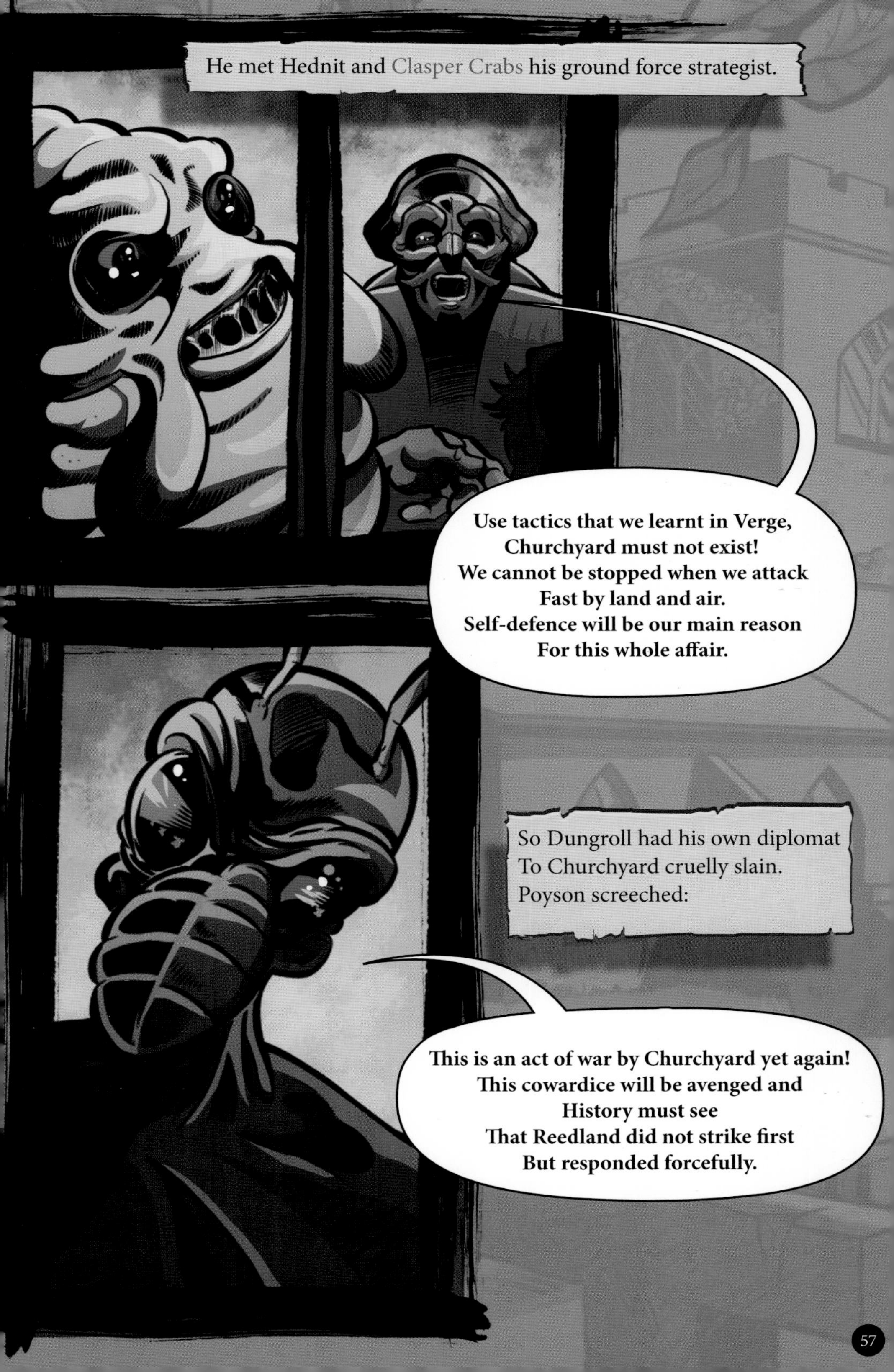

He met Hednit and Clasper Crabs his ground force strategist.
Use tactics that we learnt in Verge, Churchyard must not exist! We cannot be stopped when we attack Fast by land and air. Self-defence will be our main reason For this whole affair.
So Dungroll had his own diplomat To Churchyard cruelly slain. Poyson screeched:
This is an act of war by Churchyard yet again! This cowardice will be avenged and History must see That Reedland did not strike first But responded forcefully.

News of the threat reached Sandbank who were allies of Churchyard,
And Rock, allies of Sandbank, formed another bodyguard.
Dann De Leon of Sandbank and Rock's Spirac Nesterwing
Visited Dungroll to give him a gentle warning.

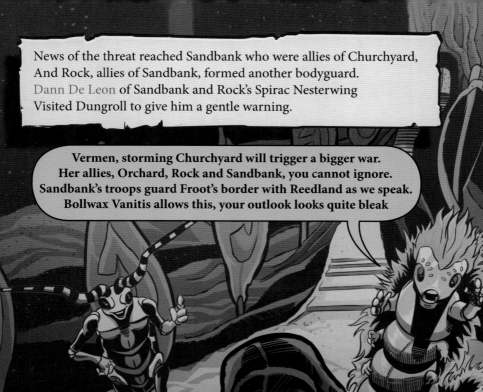

Vermen, storming Churchyard will trigger a bigger war.
Her allies, Orchard, Rock and Sandbank, you cannot ignore.
Sandbank's troops guard Froot's border with Reedland as we speak.
Bollwax Vanitis allows this, your outlook looks quite bleak

Dann and Spirac don't forget that
I have allies too.
Lilypad, Froot and Mulberry
To name but just a few.

But Vermen they are small compared to Churchyard's combined force.
Dann and I are here to guide you down another course.
Rock prepares for war, she has commenced evacuation
Of grubs to remote zones to spare her next generation.
There is a wave of opinion against us which is borne
By Rock's opposition clan leader whose name is Mite Longhorn.
My status as Rock's Leaderbug weakens by the hour,
I do not know how long I can keep Mite Longhorn from power.
If he gets in, be sure that he will fight you all the way.
Let us all agree to keep our swarms out of mortal affray.

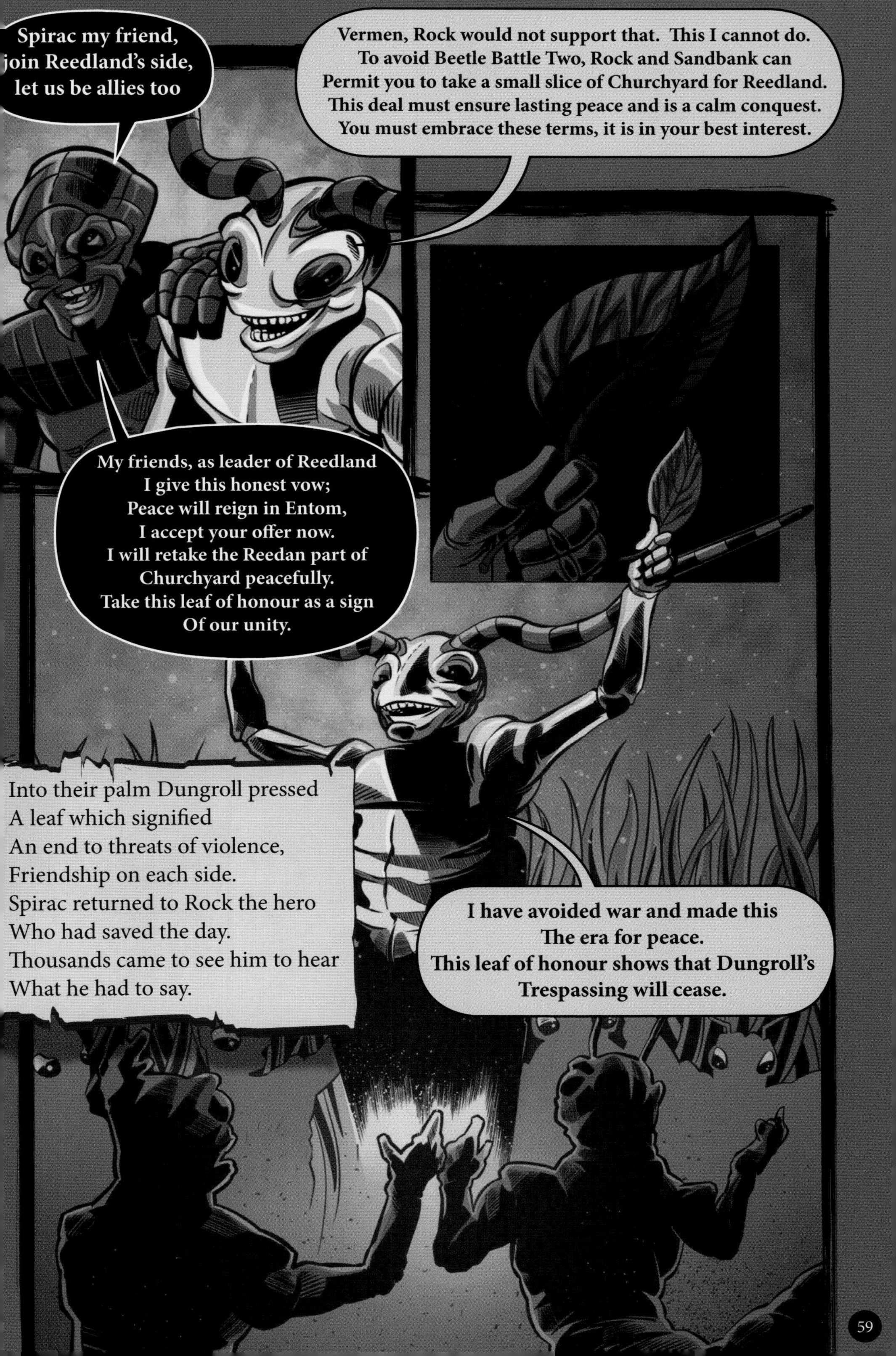
Spirac my friend, join Reedland's side, let us be allies too
Vermen, Rock would not support that. This I cannot do. To avoid Beetle Battle Two, Rock and Sandbank can Permit you to take a small slice of Churchyard for Reedland. This deal must ensure lasting peace and is a calm conquest. You must embrace these terms, it is in your best interest.
My friends, as leader of Reedland I give this honest vow; Peace will reign in Entom, I accept your offer now. I will retake the Reedan part of Churchyard peacefully. Take this leaf of honour as a sign Of our unity.
Into their palm Dungroll pressed
A leaf which signified
An end to threats of violence,
Friendship on each side.
Spirac returned to Rock the hero
Who had saved the day.
Thousands came to see him to hear
What he had to say.
I have avoided war and made this The era for peace. This leaf of honour shows that Dungroll's Trespassing will cease.

Meantime Churchyard abandoned by her allies was attacked
By neighbours Meadow and Mulberry who left Churchyard ransacked.
Her queen was forced from power and she flew quickly to Rock.
Then Churchyard had to brace herself for Dungroll's massive shock.
He went further than agreed and all of Churchyard was seized,
Leaving Dann and Spirac's deal dead and both of them displeased.
While Rock's leader catered to Dungroll, Mite Longhorn did not.
He warned Entom against the Fangs, loudly and quite a lot.
He came from noble ancestry and had held many roles
In Rock's government and military and was popular in the polls.

A great menace stirs in Entom.
We must all beware,
For war is coming. Our defences
We must now prepare.

For ladybirds and red ants distress was widespread.
One ladybird escaped Reedland and to Sandbank he fled.
There he had Reedland's ambassador assassinated.
Grimmstone raged:

Ladybird land must be obliterated.
My WETA shall destroy their Rosebush,
Their leaders must be
Arrested, sent to termite mounds,
Forced from society.
Remove all of their property.
All Fang supporters must
Rise up, destroy their roses, grind them
Down into the dust.

WETA carried out their duty with cold efficiency,
Crushing ladybirds in Rosebush most expediently.
During this Night of Broken Roses, ladybirds were lice.
For the act of one, Grimmstone made all pay a heavy price.

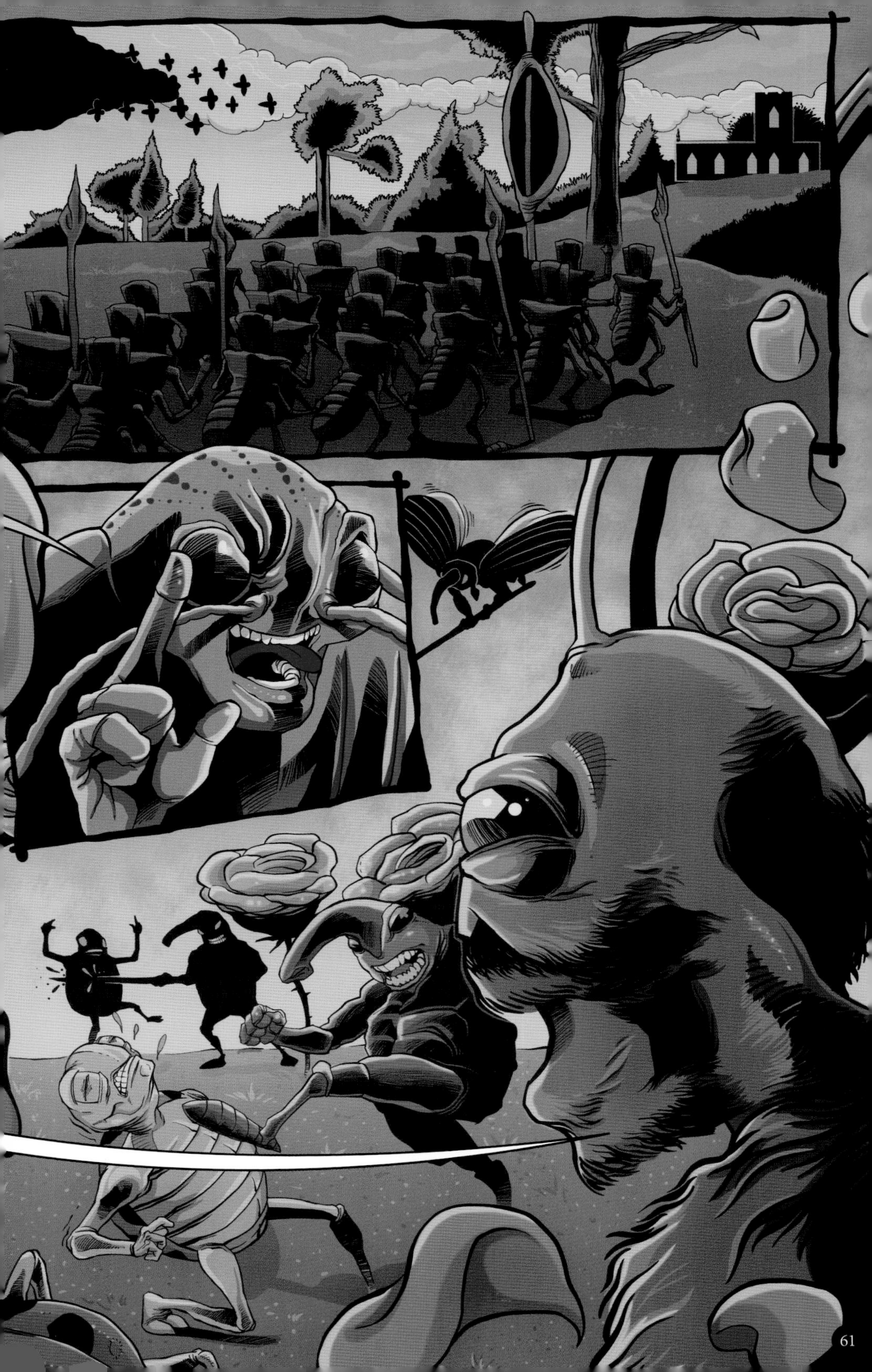

Dungroll now sought to conquer Meadow which bordered Reedland.
Churchyard's coup was bloodless but Meadow's trauma would be planned.
It would start battles throughout Entom, Dungroll knew his facts;
This was due to various covenants and friendship pacts.
Meadow had been mighty for decades but lately had been
Conquered and carved by her neighbours, her land then shared between
Reedland, Aridland and Redanta who masterminded this.
When Reedland lost Beetle Battle Meadow resurfaced.
She was sliced from the rump of Reedland by a Treaty clause.
This angered Reedland giving Dungroll goals for future wars.

Dungroll sent his swarm eastward to the border with Meadow.
This was noticed by Rock and Sandbank whose irritation showed.
Spirac Nesterwing proclaimed that Rock and Sandbank would both lend
Meadow help if Reedland invaded:

We shall all defend!

Hearing this, Dungroll was furious:

Reedland is peaceful!
We do not fear Rock or Sandbank,
They are not powerful!

Dungroll forged ahead with secret plans to take back Meadow.
Named Operation Whitefly, Dungroll's troops were set to go.
Ground force leader, Clasper Crabs, advised a strike quite soon:

While Meadow's air force is scattered and things are opportune.
They have brown butterflies and lacewings, a pathetic swarm.
No wasps, no ants, no formic acid, they are ripe to storm.
We must destroy the swarms of Rock and Sandbank from the fight.
That will be swift since they are no match for our Reedan might!

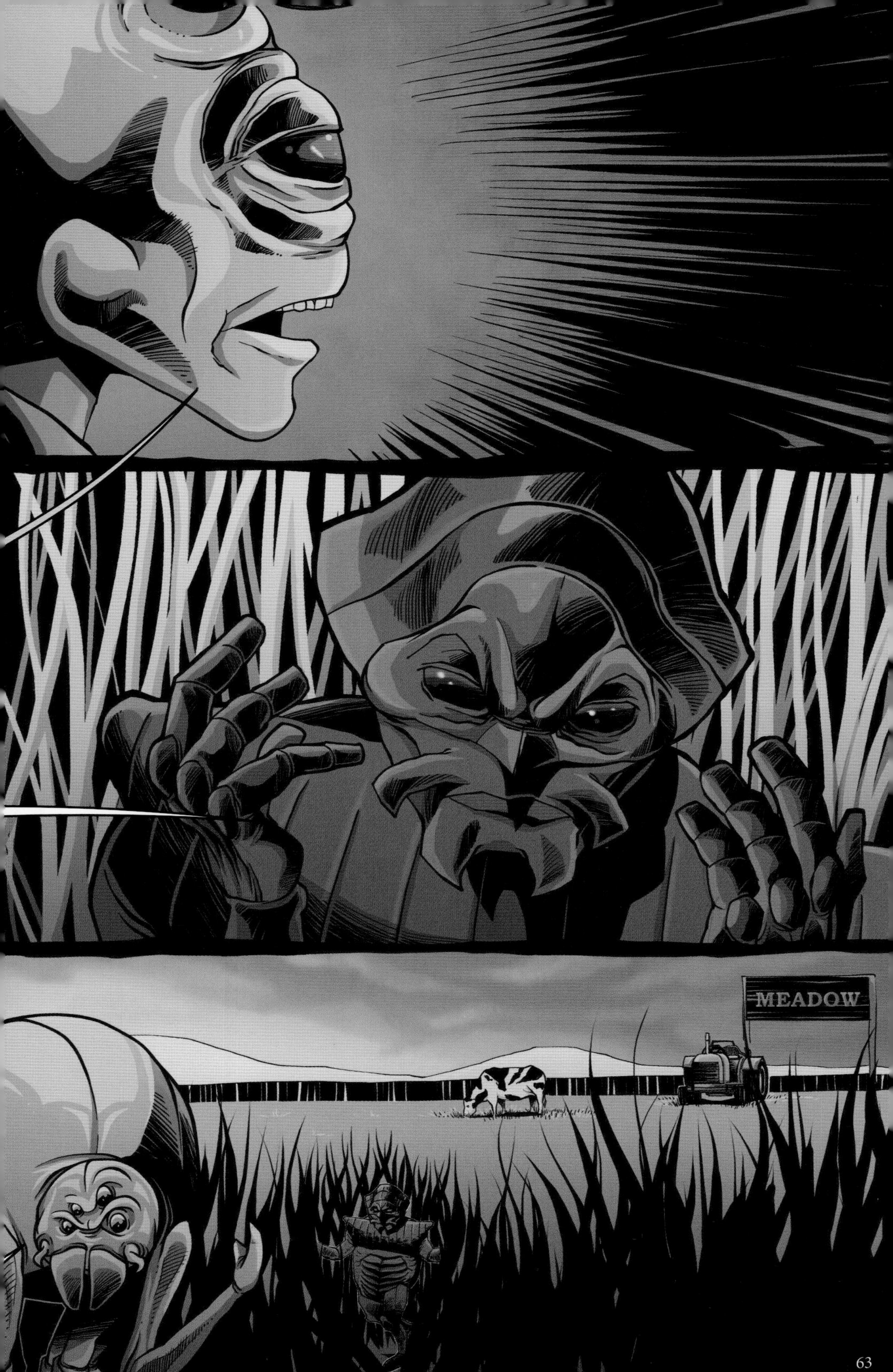
MEADOW

Meanwhile Dungroll had started peace talks with the enemy;
Boggum Biter had been sent into Mosqoto's territory.
Redanta Colonia was the destination for Biter,
His role to make the heavy weight on Dungroll much lighter.

Mosqoto was a giant of the savage revolution
Which had ended with the Queen of Redanta's brutal execution.
His battles did not end there, more slaughtering did follow.
He commanded troops in Redanta's war with the rampant Meadow.
Promotion gained him influence and status in his clan
Then when his leader died, Mosqoto's power quest began.
After heads had been removed and their twitching bodies cleared
He became Redanta's leader; opponents 'disappeared'.
Sympathy he lacked, he was suspicious of all kind.
Nature herself could not predict his dark and complex mind.
A face part-bristled with orange and brown hairs he did don
As if small woolly bears had congregated thereupon.
He was in build quite sizeable and spoke with a flat tone.
The list of those he had ordered dead was certainly full-grown.
He had a thousand assassins but Blu Mantid was best.
Blu had killed six thousand, one by one, at Mosqoto's behest.
Each of those newly headless victims had all swiftly been
Dispatched cleanly, left wriggling and followed with a preen.

The red ants' untimely exit from Beetle Battle to
Pursue their revolution saw Reedland's war fall through.
This angered many Reedans, especially Dungroll
Who was prepared to banish these thoughts to achieve his goal.
Dungroll sought peace with Redanta to stop her racing to
The aid of Rock, Sandbank or Meadow when war waged anew.

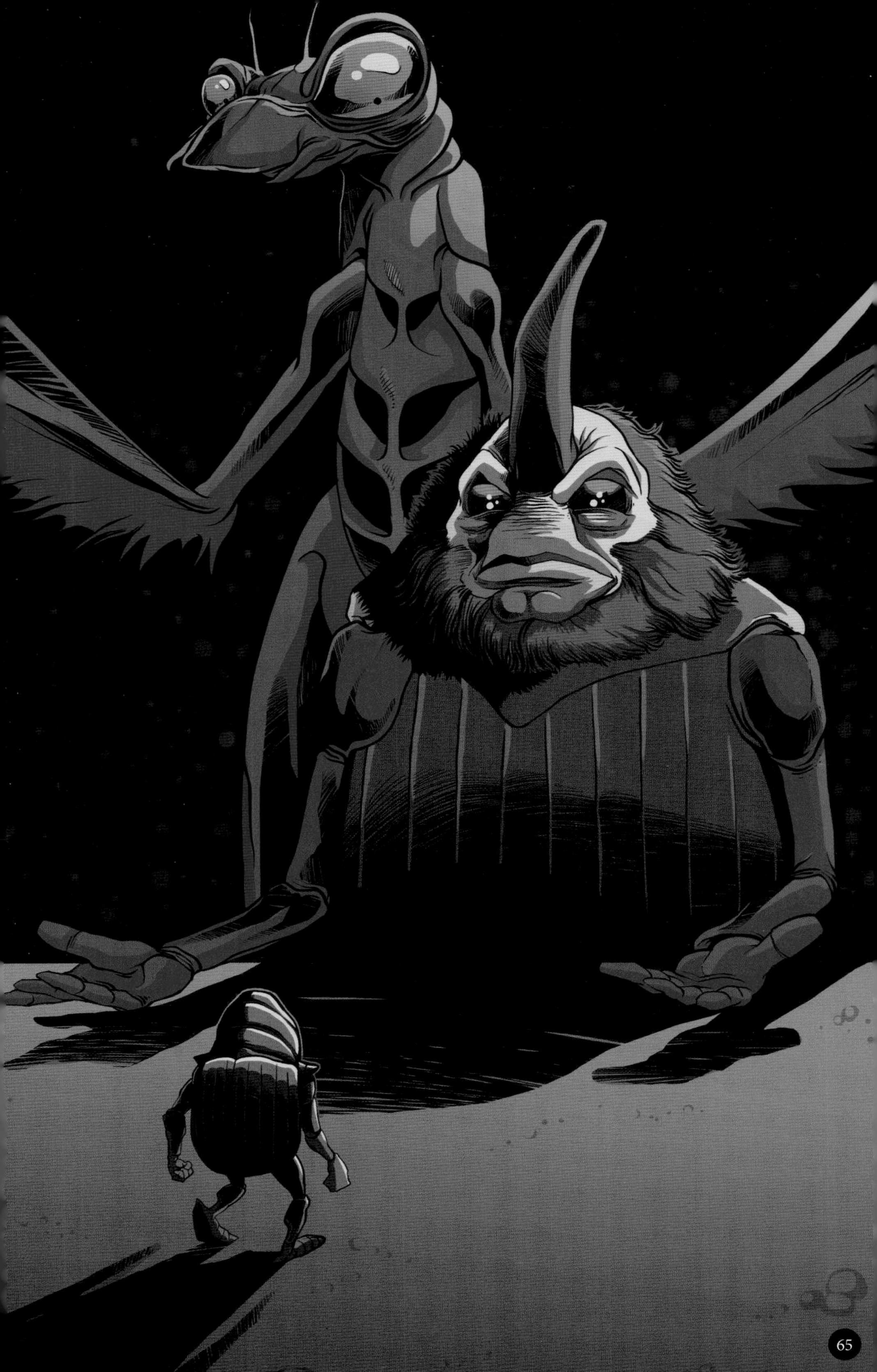

On arrival, Boggum was taken to the Myrmikka.
This was the palace of Mosqoto, his seat of power.
It was magnificently carved out underneath an old oak tree,
With beautiful chambers and corridors structured masterly.
Its ceiling dotted with fireflies and neon microbes
Illuminated every room with wonderful blue strobes.

**Boggum Biter you are most welcome,
Of that there is no doubt.**

Biter turned to see a beetle who carried a lot of clout.
It was Raspan Bloodfire who was Mosqoto's trusty
Ambassador for meddling in foreign policy.
He rose to power with Mosqoto and approved the purge.
An active red ant clansbug, it was he who caused the surge
In the thousands of swarm members cleansed, for he wrote the list
Of those to be killed, their location, who must not be missed.

Now here he was with other clansbugs from the military
And the Chief of the secret police, Lasius Rabie
Who had much power and carried out Mosqoto's decrees;
His agents slaughtered tens of thousands of political enemies.

Convolvulus Vormica was there too, the grand Head of Defence.
He was Mosqoto's closest ally, his power was immense.
Vormica joined the red ants at the same time as Bloodfire.
He stuck close to Mosqoto and helped him to rise higher.
He was involved in the purges too and when suspects were caught
And killed, it was to Vormica that their severed heads were brought.

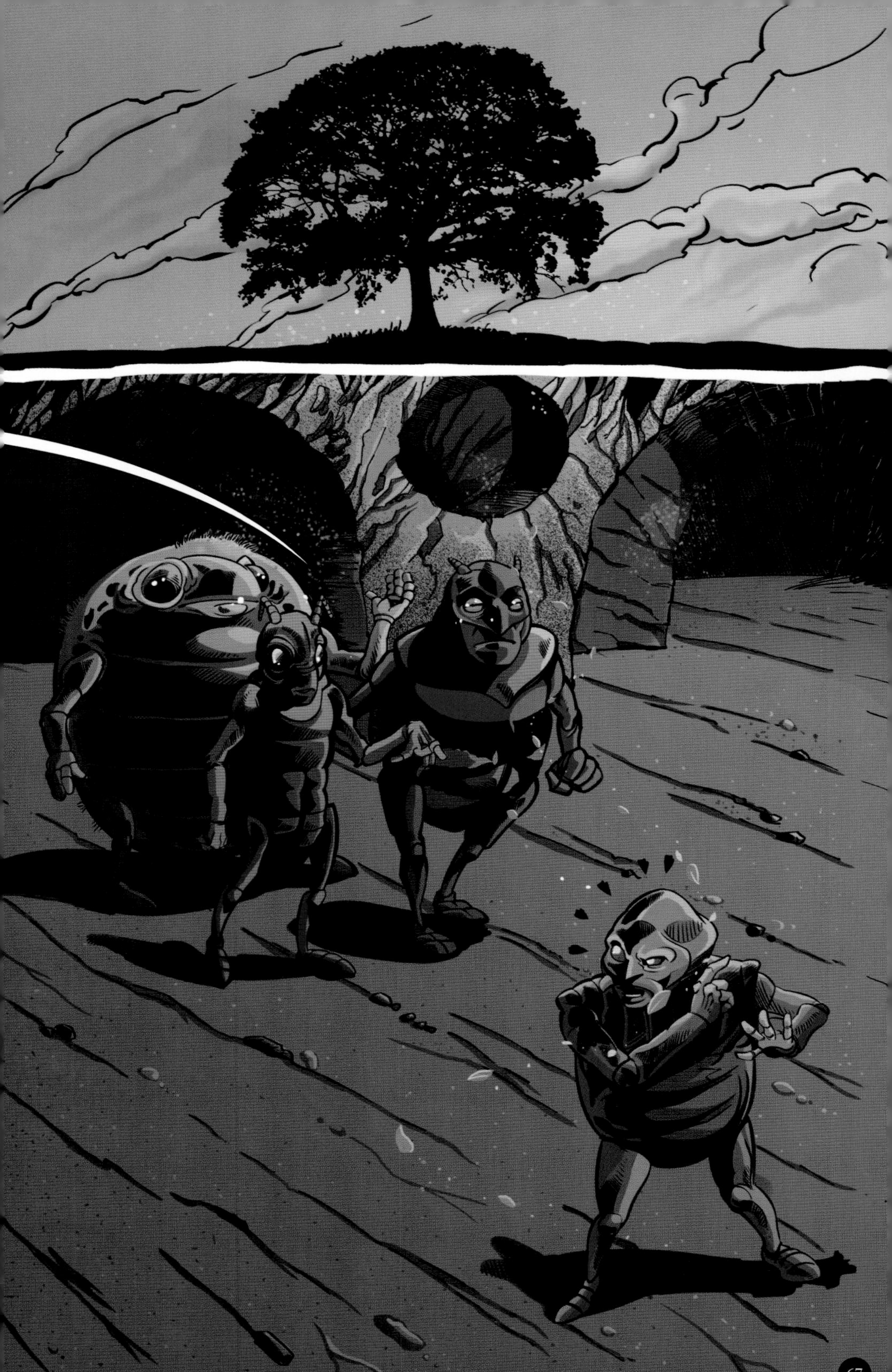

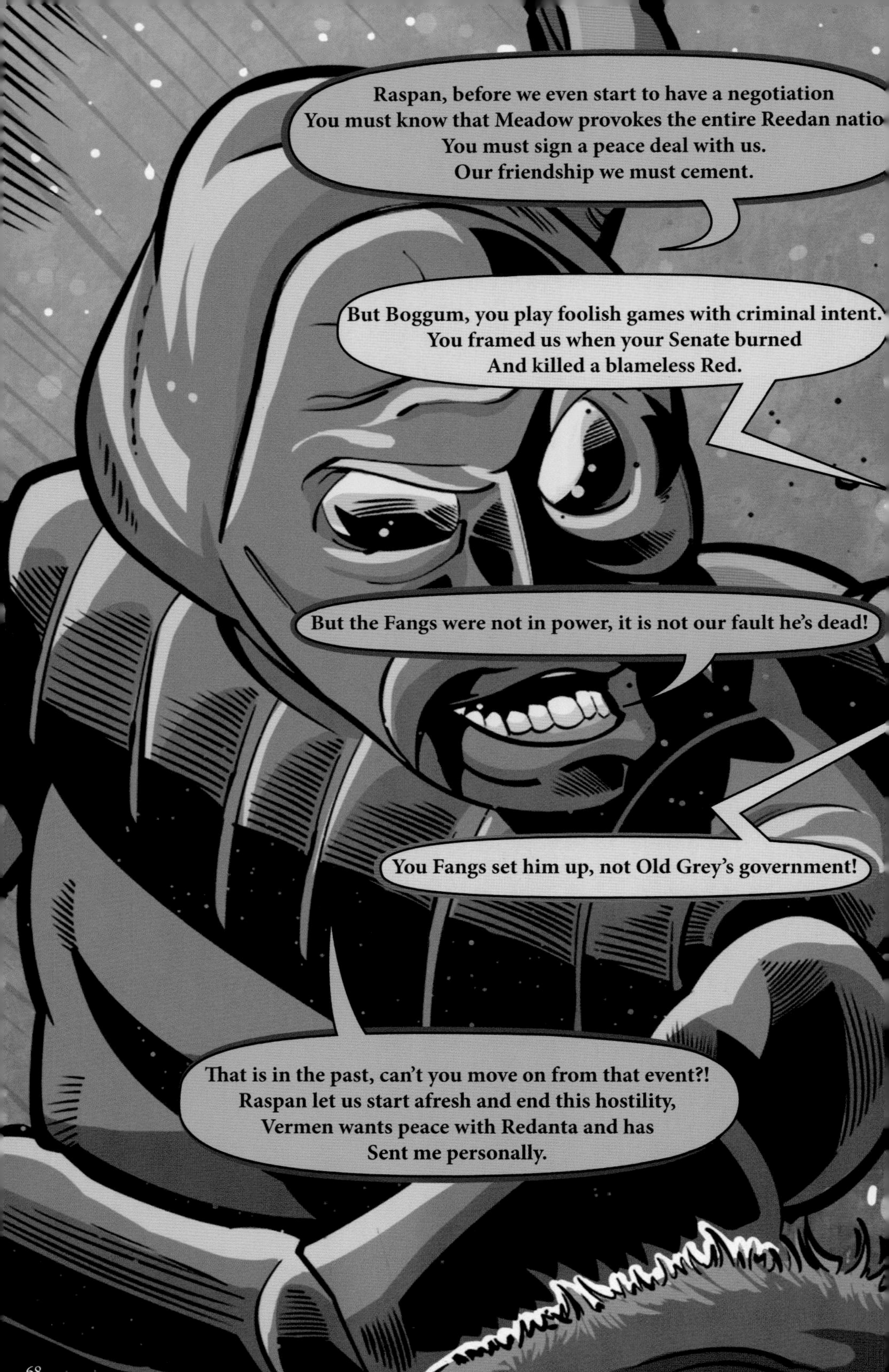
Raspan, before we even start to have a negotiation You must know that Meadow provokes the entire Reedan natio You must sign a peace deal with us. Our friendship we must cement.
But Boggum, you play foolish games with criminal intent. You framed us when your Senate burned And killed a blameless Red.
But the Fangs were not in power, it is not our fault he's dead!
You Fangs set him up, not Old Grey's government!
That is in the past, can't you move on from that event?! Raspan let us start afresh and end this hostility, Vermen wants peace with Redanta and has Sent me personally.

Lasius, Ambassador Biter
Has travelled a long way
And is a high-ranking Fang,
Not some new grub of the day.
Although Biter is a fool and
Acts imperiously,
Rock sent a larvae to us,
Dungroll behaves seriously.

I agree with you Convolvulus,
Rock and Sandbank know
If we have a pact with them,
Reedland will not attack Meadow.
Rock and Sandbank will not fight,
We will be their slave in the region.
We will not do their dirty work,
We are not their foreign legion!
Scarab Mosqoto wants us to do
This pact with Dungroll.
Let us seal this deal,
Get what we want
And take full control.

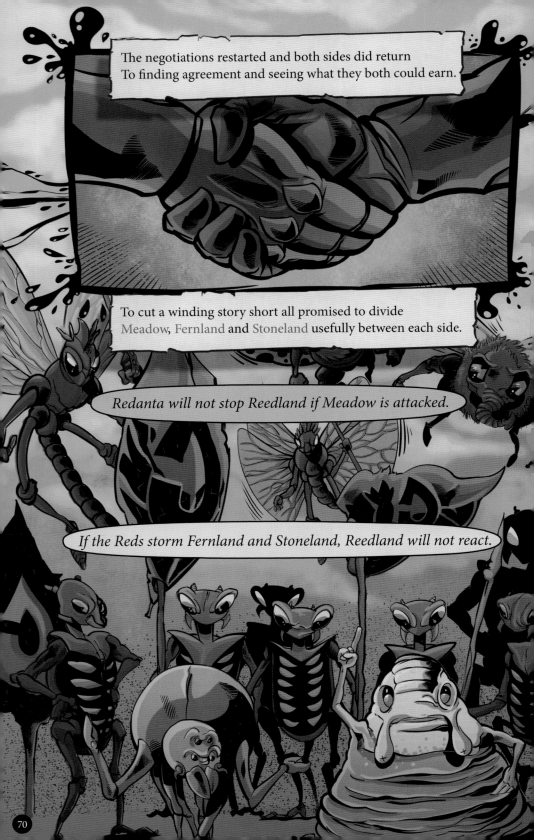

The negotiations restarted and both sides did return
To finding agreement and seeing what they both could earn.

To cut a winding story short all promised to divide
Meadow, Fernland and Stoneland usefully between each side.

Redanta will not stop Reedland if Meadow is attacked.

If the Reds storm Fernland and Stoneland, Reedland will not react.

It was a perfect deal for all involved
And Biter returned
To Reedland to give Dungroll
The good news that he had yearned.

The ecstatic Dungroll got Poyson to
Broadcast that Meadow
Had attacked Reedland, killing many,
Dealing a big blow.

Meadow's swarm lines our border, their menace is on the increase.
We have no choice, we must defend as they have rejected peace!

Dungroll ordered General Crabs to make ready the Grundsvarm
And told Hednit to get the Waerozan set to perform.

At sunlight Operation Whitefly began at great speed.
The Waerozan fizzed overhead, the Grundsvarm a stampede.
All raced to Meadow whose ground swarm was slain with quick dispatch.
Meadow defended valiantly but this was a mismatch.
The Meadow's age-old fighting methods used a cavalry
Of grasshoppers in the field springing at the enemy.
They also used brown butterflies which flew slowly and low
But neither coped with the tactics that Dungroll had on show.
His was a new attack method that Entom had not seen;
Countless hard-cased tiger beetles, spirited, brisk and mean,
Supported by dragonfly, hornet, wasp and mason bee.
The Reedans took Gräze which was Meadow's capital city.
Retreating Meadow bugs destroyed their flowers to prevent
The nectar being used to fuel this Waerozan torment.
Hednit Grubb soon ruled the airspace and Clasper Crabs the land
As Meadow's shattered forces prepared for a final stand.

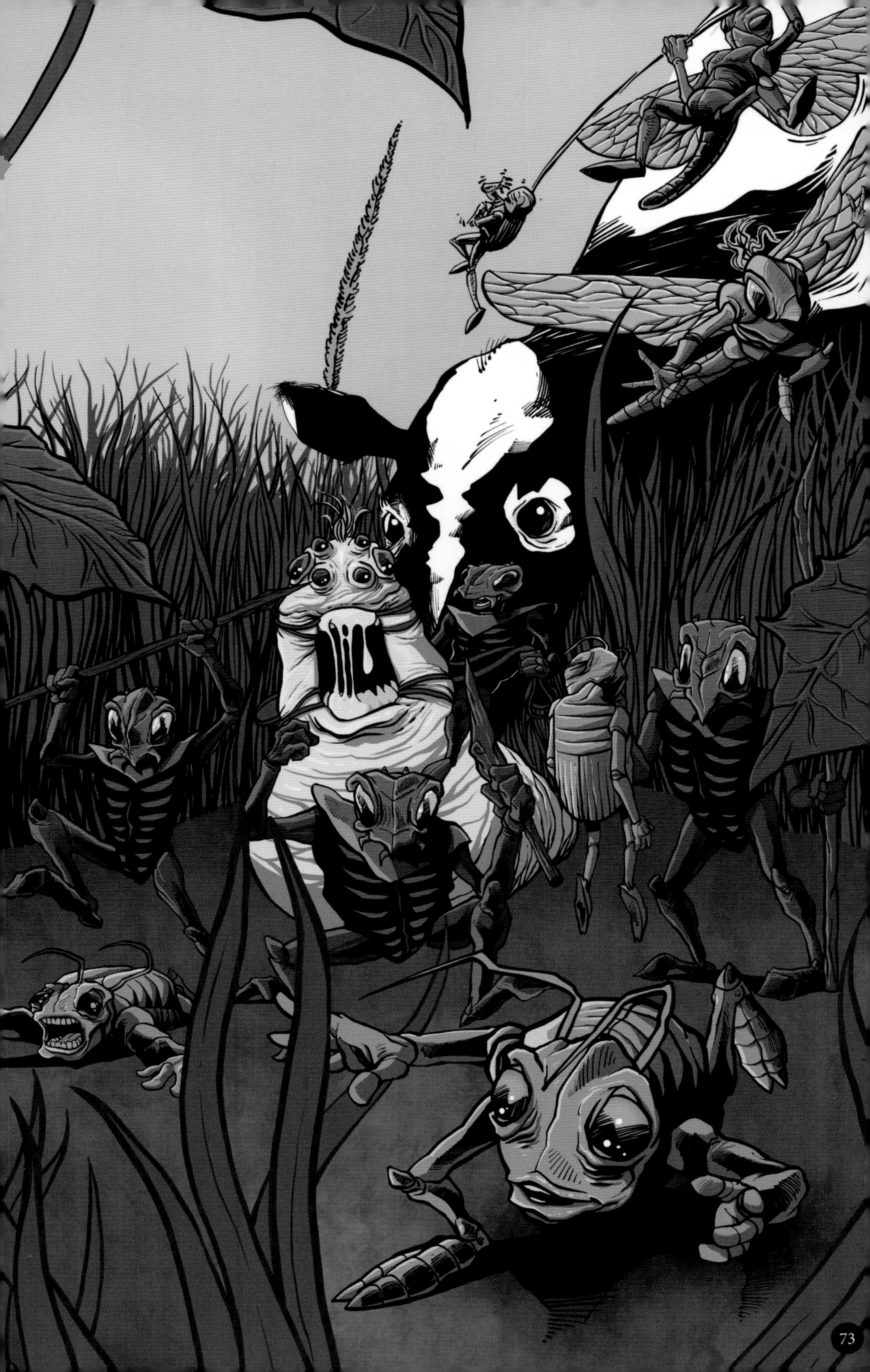

This attack sent shockwaves through Entom, Reedans were racked with pain
When they discovered that Dungroll had brought war once again.
Rock and Sandbank warned Reedland that they would join the fight
To free Meadow from the Fang noose around her which was tight.
In the Rockan Forum the weakening Spirac Nesterwing
Was criticised by Mite Longhorn for frankly dithering.

You sold Churchyard to Reedland and you made a big pledge to
Support Meadow if attacked and that is what you must do.
You waved Dungroll's leaf of honour and claimed it would bring peace
It has brought war and we must prepare for Meadow's release.
Sandbank has prepared her swarm and is now ready to act.
We must go with her for we have all signed a friendship pact.

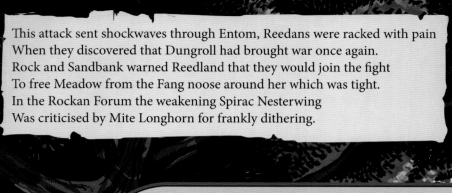

The Forum was rowdy, Nesterwing was so concerned.
The mood of Rockan citizens had very quickly turned.

But I have talked with Sandbank each and every day.
Reedland will get an ultimatum to stop now or pay.
If they do not leave the Meadow then they will be destroyed.
Our victory over them in battle would surely be enjoyed.

The next day in Pollen, Reedland's capital, shrieks pierced the air.
Something had given everyone an almighty scare.
News had reached them from Rock which had caused them to shriek more.
Against Reedland the Rockans declared that they were at war.
Sandbank had joined them, diplomatic routes no longer run.
Dungroll's bluff was called and **BEETLE BATTLE TWO BEGUN!**

Chapter 4
Beetle Battle Two

Dungroll did not want this despite his threats and power show.
He railed at his henchbugs for failing to prevent this woe.

You said they would not fight us and that
They were not ready.
Your intelligence was wrong,
You have failed me totally!
The Rock is an island, surround it
With a deadly ring
Of U-Bugs and fliers to stop all
Supplies entering.
Nothing must cross the Pond because of
Our steadfast blockade
Then when the time is right for us
The Rock we shall invade!

In Rock, though war was due, a peaceful period began;
The calm before the storm, a peculiar timespan.
No buzz, strafing nor invasion by Waerozan or swarm.
It was as if nothing had happened, things seemed of the norm.
Pollination continued by the bee and butterfly,
Earthworms bored tunnels, ticks drank blood, fleas took to the sky.

In the hives and nests of Reedland
The clawsmith and chemist
Produced weaponry to strike nations
On Dungroll's blacklist.
Stings, acids and fighter bugs
Were produced at great rate.
Hornets and armies of ants
Were those weapons of hate.
Damselflies joined the Waerozan,
U-Bugs formed a crew
Of diving beetles, water boatmen,
Dragonfly nymphs too.

Meadow fell to the Reedans and to Rock her queen did flee.
Mosqoto's red ants entered Meadow plundering freely.
The red ants also swallowed Flatland, Stoneland and Leafland.
Mosqoto was jubilant at the success he had planned.

Comrades, that germ infested Dungroll has no idea.
Today we have greatly expanded mighty Redanta.
Half of Meadow is now ours and will act as a buffer
Between us and Reedland; to get this no Reds did suffer.
No red ant lives were lost in taking the eastern Meadow
But the west is littered with empty shells of their Reedan foe.

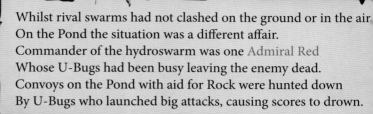

Whilst rival swarms had not clashed on the ground or in the air,
On the Pond the situation was a different affair.
Commander of the hydroswarm was one Admiral Red
Whose U-Bugs had been busy leaving the enemy dead.
Convoys on the Pond with aid for Rock were hunted down
By U-Bugs who launched big attacks, causing scores to drown.

A Reedan dragonfly nymph made her stealthy way along
The bed of the Pond and launched a mighty ambush upon
The Rockan water boatmen fleet as they lay in port;
Striking fear through Rock's heart, a wartime lesson had been taught.
A delighted Dungroll said this act was the moment when
Rock's era of empire did close and Reedland's did open.
The Rockan fleet was the reason why Rock had gained her empire,
She ruled the Pond and knew well how to conquer and acquire.
Her colonies spread throughout Entom and above it all
She was feared and lauded and her queen was known by great and small.

Grimmstone meantime was busy planning
The next stage of strife.
For Meadow's ladybirds he decreed:

Reedland owns your life!
You will be controlled, work for Reedland
And must all live in
The dungy earth of a pig farm
And feast on beast dropping.

Vermen, let me give you more
Details of this master plan.
No one uses ladybird labour
As well as I can.
The ultimate resolution to
The problem shall be
Eradication of ladybirds
Done efficiently.

Pox and I have built termite mounds
In the west of Meadow.
The disused molehill mountains are where
Some shall also go.

We'll send them there in numbers
That have not been seen before.
course they will be disposed of when
They can work no more.

Next, Scarab Mosqoto ordered the storming of Fernland.

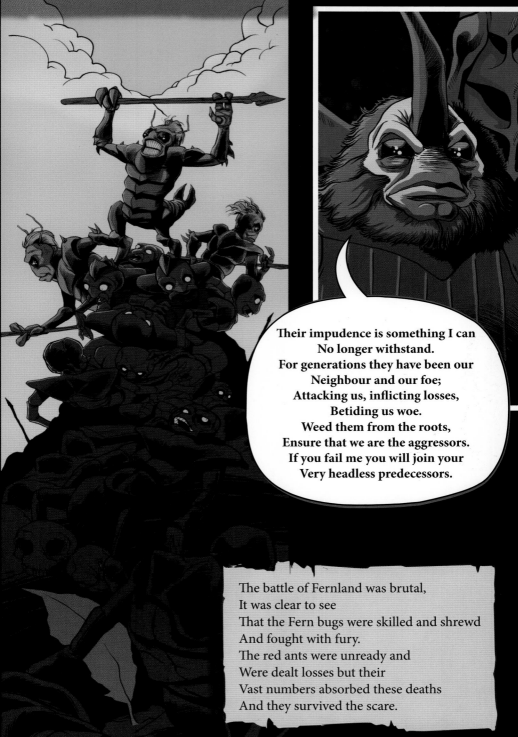

Their impudence is something I can
No longer withstand.
For generations they have been our
Neighbour and our foe;
Attacking us, inflicting losses,
Betiding us woe.
Weed them from the roots,
Ensure that we are the aggressors.
If you fail me you will join your
Very headless predecessors.

The battle of Fernland was brutal,
It was clear to see
That the Fern bugs were skilled and shrewd
And fought with fury.
The red ants were unready and
Were dealt losses but their
Vast numbers absorbed these deaths
And they survived the scare.

Redanta went on to win but their poor performance was
Noted by Dungroll who said:

It was simply because
Of the cull Mosqoto did of his swarm quite recently.
The Ferns have exposed his folly and shortly so shall we.
If I had known that the red ants were not ready for war
I would have attacked them by now, of that you can be sure.
We must control all routes from bed to surface of the Pond.
Our hydroswarm is ready to siege Rock and far beyond.
To control the Pond we need harbours in Barge and Ducknest.
Once we have that, the coming war will not be a contest.
Ducknest is small and borders our most northern tip and will
Be quick to conquer for their swarm lacks size, hunger and skill.

Ducknest looked on nervously as a Reedan water crew
Grew slowly, larger, closer and aggressive in their view.
Then without warning, Admiral Red's hydroswarm attacked.
Hordes of U-Bugs rose up and Ducknest was soon ransacked.

The fall of Ducknest was swift and the next target loomed large;
A short distance from Reedland lay the Republic of Barge.
The Fangs invaded Barge with their best fighters straightaway.
Wasps carried the Siafu there to enter the fray.
Resistance here was stiffer though, Barge was not to be
Destroyed by Reedland's air nor land force expeditiously.
Dungroll sent a screech beetle to demand that Barge lays down
Her arms and that Her Majesty removes her royal crown.
The Queen of Barge had no intention of surrendering;
Urging her swarm to fight the Fangs and never to give in.
Dungroll was enraged by her refusal to capitulate
So he ordered:

More fire, more attacks.
We must seal her fate.
Crush her, her royal court and chambers.
Every trace must go!
Since she will not submit to me,
She dies a fool's hero!

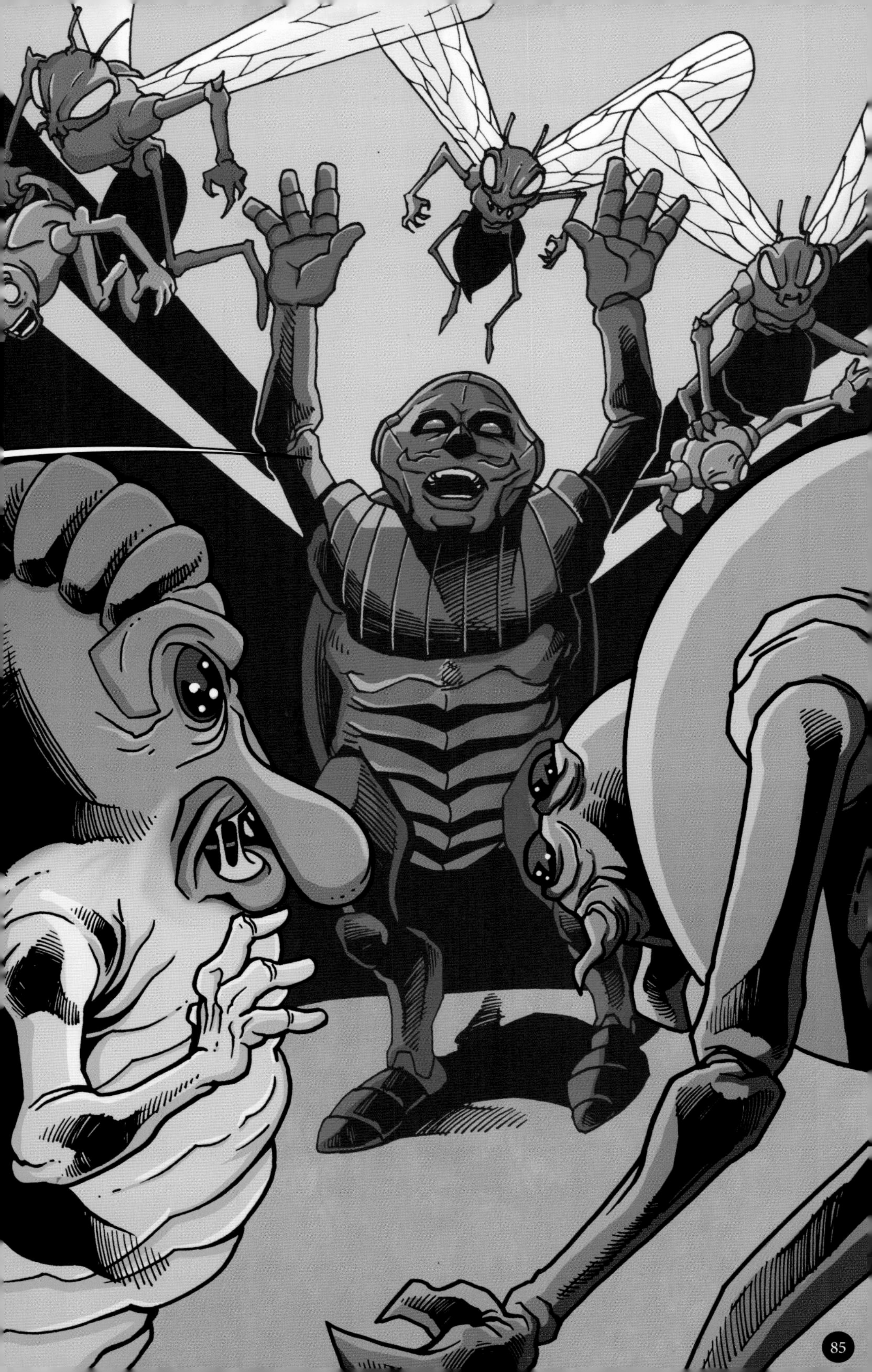

At once a squad of hornets entered, whirring overhead.
Spiderlings parachuted down on wafted silken threads.

Rock, fearing the endgame for Barge, did form a rescue plan;
Nesterwing rushed some maybugs there to repel the Waerozan.
It was Rock's first fight of the war and side by side with Barge,
Both hopelessly outnumbered to prevent the Reedan charge.
The rescue plan was failing against Reedland's swarm elite,
Continuous Waerozan dive-bombing forced them to retreat.
Pushed back to the city of Stern, bewildered and in shock,
Some Rockans plucked the Queen from harm and fled with her to Rock.
The rest were stung by hunter wasps which paralysed them and
Flew their limp but live bodies back to feed the fatherland.
Barge surrendered shortly afterwards, Dungroll now had all
The harbours needed for Pond control and for Rock's downfall.

Wild celebrations marked the passage of more territory
Into Reedland's empire; Dungroll now boasted gleefully.

First Aridland then Churchyard, Garden, Meadow and Ducknest;
Now Barge, it will not take us long to conquer all the rest.
Hednit and Clasper the joint air-land strikes work well at speed.
I want you both to invade Gravel but first conquer Tweed.

Wedged between Gravel and Reedland was the wetland Tweed.
It merged with the Pond and was a short swim from Rock indeed.
Its waters had five towers of feathered grass reaching high,
Which were great cities of little beasts from midges to blackfly.
During the First Beetle Battle, Tweed was a neutral zone.
Whilst Gravel and Reedland waged war, Tweed remained all alone.
It shared peace with Reedland and at the end of that war
The Reedan monarch fled there, the empire was no more.
The Waerozan flew to Tweed with a screeched message which said:

"Bugs of Tweed do not be alarmed, you are protected
By the air and land swarms of Reedland against an attack
From Rock and Sandbank. If they strike we'll send the cowards back!"

During the First Beetle Battle, Tweed had heard this before,
Reedland promised to protect her but invaded, causing war.
History was repeating itself, it was clear to see
So Tweed did not accept Dungroll's offer immediately.
Meanwhile the pressure mounted on Rock's Spirac Nesterwing.
In the opinion polls he was taking a massive battering.
He was viewed as weakly kowtowing to every Fang whim
And in the Rockan Forum verbal stings rained down upon him.
These attacks took their toll and Spirac weakened by the hour.
Mite Longhorn now gained control, forcing Spirac out of power.

The popular Longhorn had served in Rock's mighty swarm.
He had travelled to Bramble, Woodland, Rabbit Down and had performed
Bravely in Riverside Lands in the battle of Gnarly Yew.
Then in the slaughter that was the Fen war, he had fought too.
He had held different posts in Rock's government previously;
During the First Beetle Battle he took charge of weaponry.
He had also led the hydroswarm and had seen close battle
As commander in savage clashes over war-torn Gravel.
When that conflict ended he took charge of Rock's nectary.
Now as Rock's new leader he needed another victory.

The battle for Tweed was short as the brutal Waerozan
Dropped fighters from the sky on to this unsuspecting land.
Four of the five towers of grass were breached overall
As ravenous Fang caterpillars chewed holes in their wall.
Invaders then entered the stems through this bitten slit
And raced upwards, felling defenders at the plume's summit.
The Queen of Tweed and her royal court were whisked away meanwhile;
Destination Rock to start her royal exile.

Tweed's fifth tower was a large port and a very busy city.
It was called Wisp and it was defended much more fiercely.
Resilient Tweed bugs frustrated Dungroll's attempts to gain
A swift capitulation of Tweed without loss or pain.
In desperation Dungroll threw his grasshopper platoons
At Wisp in order to force her fall by the afternoon.
The sky darkened as they arrived in waves of springs and dives.
These part-flying leapers aimed to end so many lives.
Their hunger for grass warfare gave the Fangs a key breakthrough
And saw the ominous advance of Reedland continue.
An ermine moth then flew over the grasshopper attack.
Her broad white wings signified to all fighters to hold back.
She was Entom's symbol of ceasefire and this indicated
That Reedland wanted some kind of peace deal negotiated.
Tweed paused the fighting and allowed a Fang screech beetle to
Make its way up the quill to broadcast Dungroll's point of view:

"THE SUN HAS SET ON YOUR DEFIANCE. SURRENDER NOW OR DIE."

As Tweed considered this proposal, death came from the sky.
The grasshoppers struck once again, chewing Wisp to cud
Then wasps flew past the white moth, slaying Tweed bugs in cold blood.

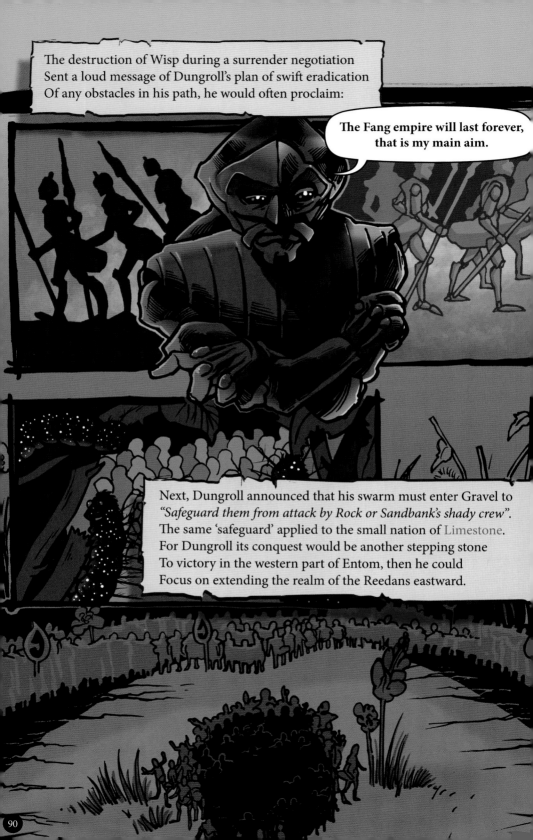

The destruction of Wisp during a surrender negotiation
Sent a loud message of Dungroll's plan of swift eradication
Of any obstacles in his path, he would often proclaim:

The Fang empire will last forever, that is my main aim.

Next, Dungroll announced that his swarm must enter Gravel to
"Safeguard them from attack by Rock or Sandbank's shady crew".
The same 'safeguard' applied to the small nation of Limestone.
For Dungroll its conquest would be another stepping stone
To victory in the western part of Entom, then he could
Focus on extending the realm of the Reedans eastward.

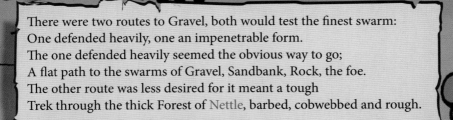

There were two routes to Gravel, both would test the finest swarm:
One defended heavily, one an impenetrable form.
The one defended heavily seemed the obvious way to go;
A flat path to the swarms of Gravel, Sandbank, Rock, the foe.
The other route was less desired for it meant a tough
Trek through the thick Forest of Nettle, barbed, cobwebbed and rough.

Dungroll chose the march through Nettle, thinking it was wise.
He planned to catch the enemy by the next sunrise.
At once, huge numbers of ground beetles entered the forest.
The thick nettles were everywhere and hampered their progress.
Their route twisted and turned as they found a way around
The hairy pillars rising up high from out of the ground.
Fang caterpillars once again proved a handy tool
As they feasted on the stinging jungle, turning it to stool.
Whilst the swarms of Gravel, Sandbank and Rock readied their frontier,
The Reedans burst through the nettles and advanced to their foes' rear.
They then fanned out and closed in on the allies from both sides.
The plan worked well and took the three swarms by complete surprise.
This massive shock showed Entom that Dungroll was well prepared.
The Reedans raced towards the Pond, the allies were ensnared.

Sandbank's reserve army failed and Dungroll took no pity.
His troops marched swiftly towards Dune, Sandbank's capital city.

Dungroll was pleased and as the Grundsvarm prepared themselves to
Wipe out the three trapped allies, the doubts in Dungroll's mind grew.
The allies were at the mercy of Clasper Crabs' swift attack.
Crabs planned to drown them in the Pond by pushing them right back.
With victory a certainty of one more Crabs assault,
Dungroll intervened and ordered the ground attack to halt.

This caused alarm for Crabs who saw flaws in Dungroll's new plan:

He wants the trapped allies destroyed just by the Waerozan!
This is insane, Grubb wants the glory but attacks by air
Won't work. Ground troops are what's needed to choke them in our snare.

Whilst debate raged on who should effect the final victory,
The Queen of Gravel surrendered to the Reedans quite tamely.
The Gravellian swarm however did fight on valiantly
Which helped the Rockan swarm with their unlikely plan to flee.
Their flight, organised by Longhorn, would be quite a feat.
His announcement detailed what was an embarrassing retreat.

The plan needs an armada to traverse the Pond and reach
Our trapped and brave ground swarm penned in on Sandbank's shingled beach.
We must evacuate them back to Rock and then liberate
Them from impending doom, we cannot leave them to their fate.

And so the strangest flotilla Entom had ever seen
Comprising insects great and small, some black, some brown, some green,
Some skating, some rowing, some swimming, some not of the norm,
Went to and back across the Pond to save Rock's trapped ground swarm.
Some called it a phenomenon, other hallowed words were used
To describe this hour when most of Rock's ground swarm were rescued.

Dungroll then quashed the halt order so Crabs attacked again.
(His language when he saw most Rockans gone was quite profane.)

The Sanden and Gravellian troops though did not get away
But they had helped Rock to escape to fight another day.
Mite Longhorn raised Rock's morale with defiant bulletins.

Much of Entom falls to the Fangs but we shall *NEVER* give in.

Sandbank capitulated and her leaders fled from Dune.
The clawko was hoisted over it later that afternoon.
Their surrender was signed in the same forest locality
That Sandbank had made Reedland sign the Surrender Treaty.

Such a sweet reversal for Dungroll, his empire restocked.
He now turned his attention to invasion of the Rock.
He called it Operation Frog for it relied upon
An amphibious attack by the Grundsvarm moving through the Pond.
Some would be parachuted in then all would join together
In Pebble, Longhorn's seat of power and force his surrender.
First Dungroll needed to destroy Rock's little air force and
Fill her skies with the many flies of his mighty Waerozan.
He hoped that Rock would see the peril of the situation
And be persuaded to commence a peace negotiation.

He summoned Clasper Crabs, Hednit Grubb and Admiral Red
To draft an invasion plan to leave Rock's defence dead.
They wanted to delay the raid, Dungroll wanted it now.
The attack plan was changed constantly, they could not agree how.
Plotting the ground invasion was a difficult case.
The Waerozan meanwhile was flying through Rockan airspace.
On the Pond surface were pondskaters bringing aid to Rock;
They formed a long convoy conveying food and other stock.
The Fang fliers dive-bombed them, dropping oily seeds from high
Which broke the water surface, sinking the convoy's supply.
They also attacked Rock's flowerbeds and targeted their hives.
Such terrifying attacks claimed many innocent lives.

On some islands of the Pond between Sandbank and Rock,
Reedland did invade leaving the citizens in shock.
They introduced new laws curtailing much activity
And restricted the freedom of the whole community.
Slave labour camps were built on Pine with thousands of resources.
Some islanders escaped to serve with Rock or Sandbank's forces.
Slaves toiled to make the larger islands heavily fortified
And many folk were executed or in prison died.

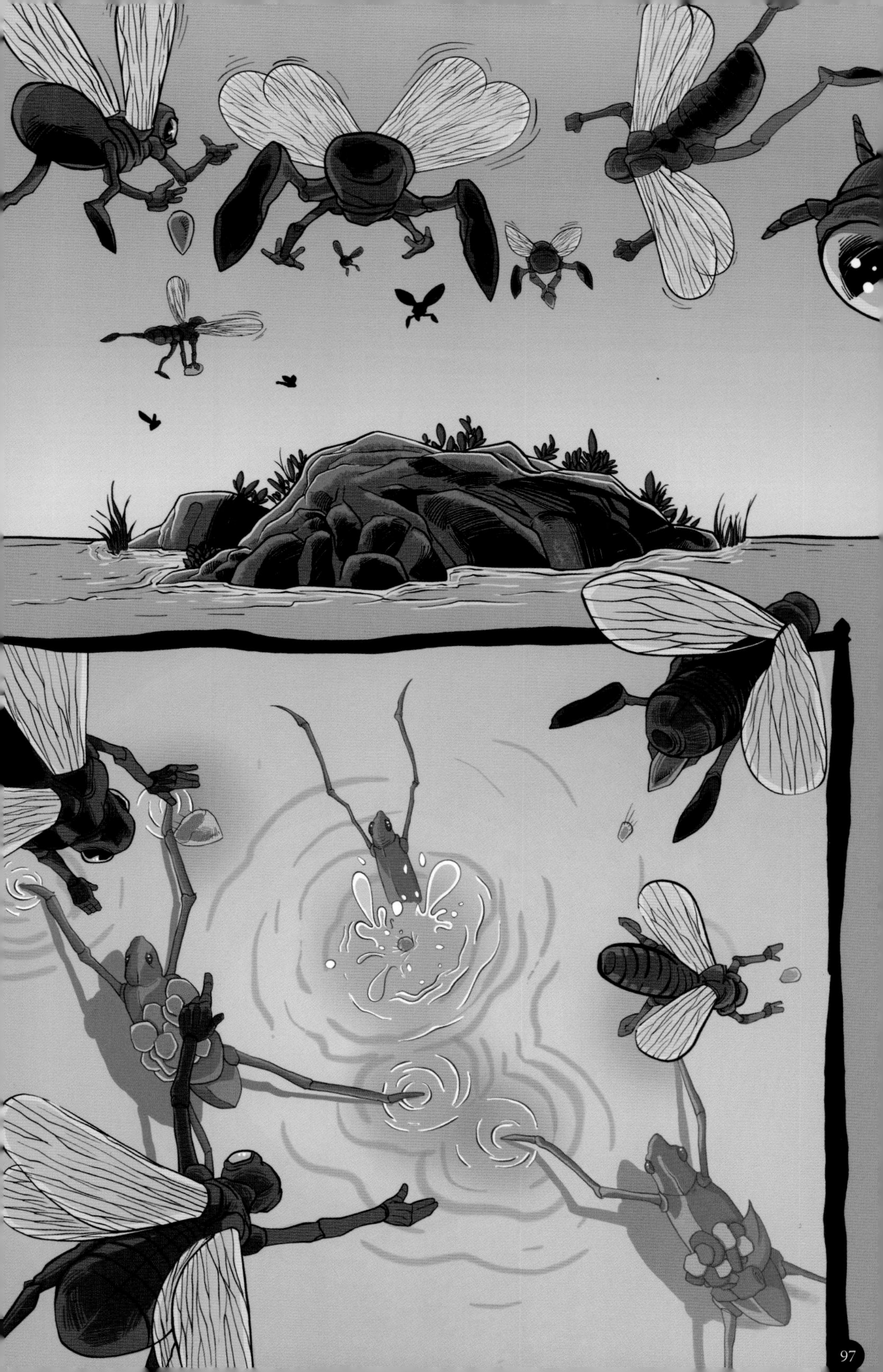

Rock's airspace though was not yet Reedan owned and occupied.
The Waerozan came under fierce attack from Rock's horseflies.
Faster and more agile than Reedland's air military,
Dogfights raged as each side sought to slay the enemy.
This took a toll on Rock's stretched fliers who had fewer resources
Than the mighty machine that made up Reedland's airborne forces.
These accurate attacks on Rock's fighters and supplies
Meant no rest for Rock's Air Command nor for her tired flies.

Rock had devised a detection system enabling herself to
Get early warning of raids by the Waerozan air crew.
The system, called N-Tenna, used moth antennae to track
Reedan squadrons then scramble horseflies to stop the attack.
N-Tenna worked, the Waerozan were swatted and dispersed
By Rock's superb horseflies once the Pond had been traversed.

A Reedan attack missed its military target one twilight
And attacked Pebble's civilians, giving all a mighty fright.
Mite Longhorn responded by sending the Rockan Air Force to
Strike Pollen for the very first time in this Beetle Battle Two.
Dungroll was incandescent, livid, seething to the core;
Grubb had promised that no attacks would ever come to Reedland's door!
Enraged, he stopped the targeting of hives and flowerbeds
And ordered Pebble to be 'wreckzed' by the Waerozan instead.
Pebble was heavily pounded by a furious bee frenzy.
For many days strong bolts of shocking stings rained constantly.
Other cities of Rock were wreckzed including the industrial Old Creek Bay
Which was sadly unrecognisable once the Waerozan had passed that way.
Death tolls, buzz storms, sirens, rations, destruction and fear,
Conditions for all citizens were dreadfully severe.

The wreckzing of Pebble did allow the Rockan Air Force to
Repair and replenish her hives, flowerbeds and brave air crew.
Despite damage to Pebble, Rock churned out many horsefly,
Rising from the water to bite the Waerozan from the sky.
Rock's nests also delivered more wasps, her hives produced more bees
So over Rock Dungroll could not gain air supremacy.
Operation Frog was cancelled. The Waerozan had lost.
The Battle of Rock was over and for Dungroll, what a cost!

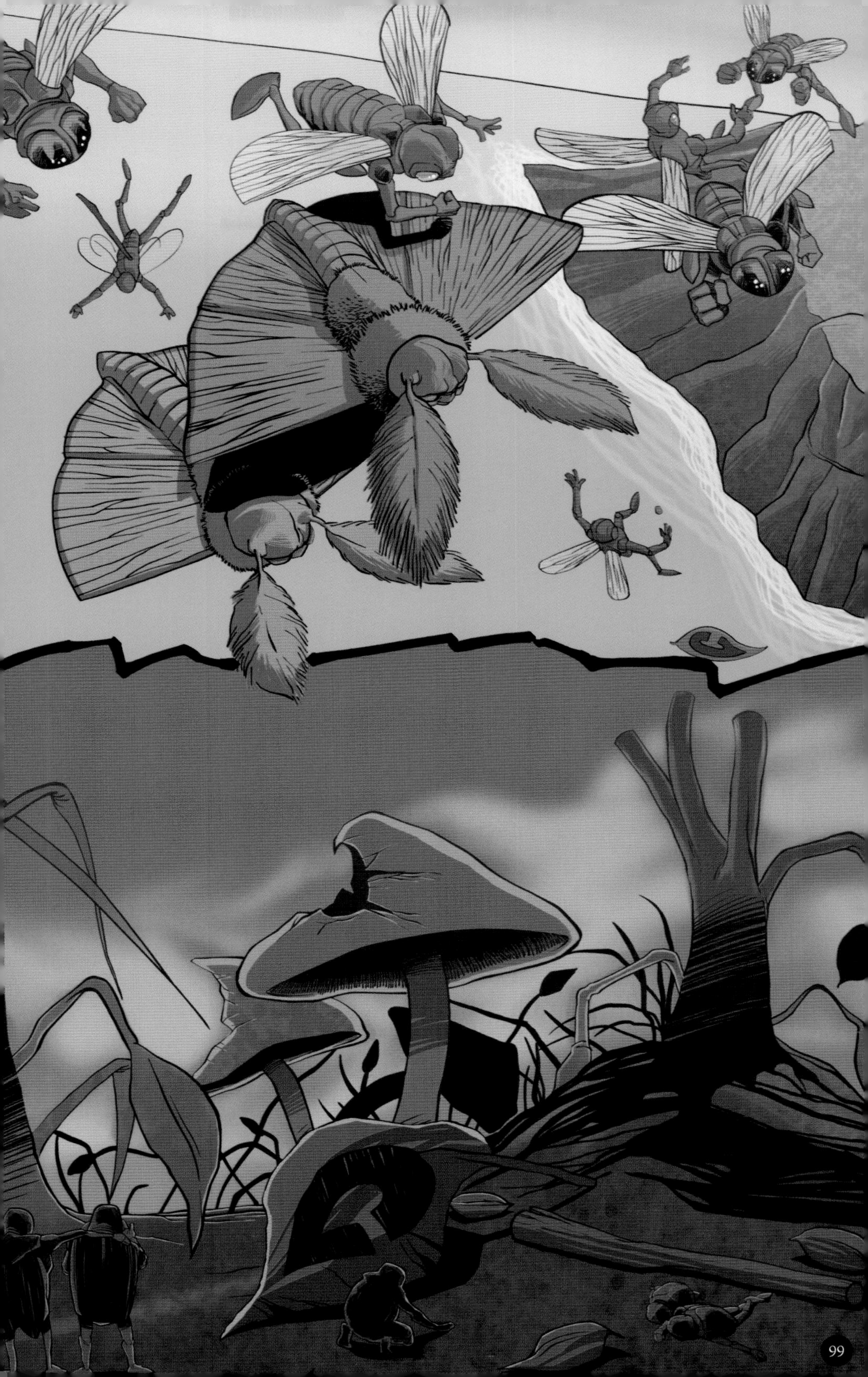

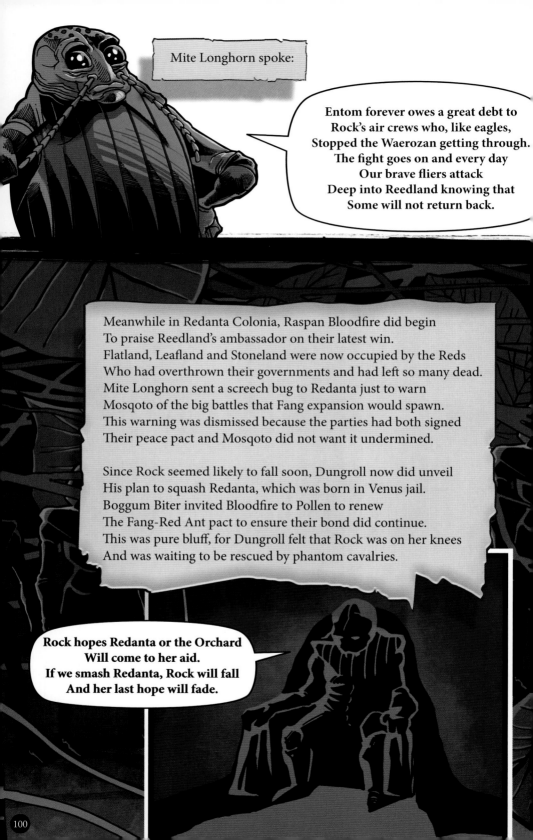

Mite Longhorn spoke:

Entom forever owes a great debt to
Rock's air crews who, like eagles,
Stopped the Waerozan getting through.
The fight goes on and every day
Our brave fliers attack
Deep into Reedland knowing that
Some will not return back.

Meanwhile in Redanta Colonia, Raspan Bloodfire did begin
To praise Reedland's ambassador on their latest win.
Flatland, Leafland and Stoneland were now occupied by the Reds
Who had overthrown their governments and had left so many dead.
Mite Longhorn sent a screech bug to Redanta just to warn
Mosqoto of the big battles that Fang expansion would spawn.
This warning was dismissed because the parties had both signed
Their peace pact and Mosqoto did not want it undermined.

Since Rock seemed likely to fall soon, Dungroll now did unveil
His plan to squash Redanta, which was born in Venus jail.
Boggum Biter invited Bloodfire to Pollen to renew
The Fang-Red Ant pact to ensure their bond did continue.
This was pure bluff, for Dungroll felt that Rock was on her knees
And was waiting to be rescued by phantom cavalries.

Rock hopes Redanta or the Orchard
Will come to her aid.
If we smash Redanta, Rock will fall
And her last hope will fade.

On the eve of the peace talks in Pollen's red ant embassy,
Biter hosted an ambassadors' ball for high society.
Bloodfire was there with an entourage of red ant diplomats.
All made merry and did bury any sign of a spat.
Biter boasted:

My dear Raspan, you know Rock is nearly finished.

Mite Longhorn's message now arrived. Rock was not diminished.
The messengers were squadrons of bees attacking from high,
Causing dignitaries to seek shelter or stay behind and die.

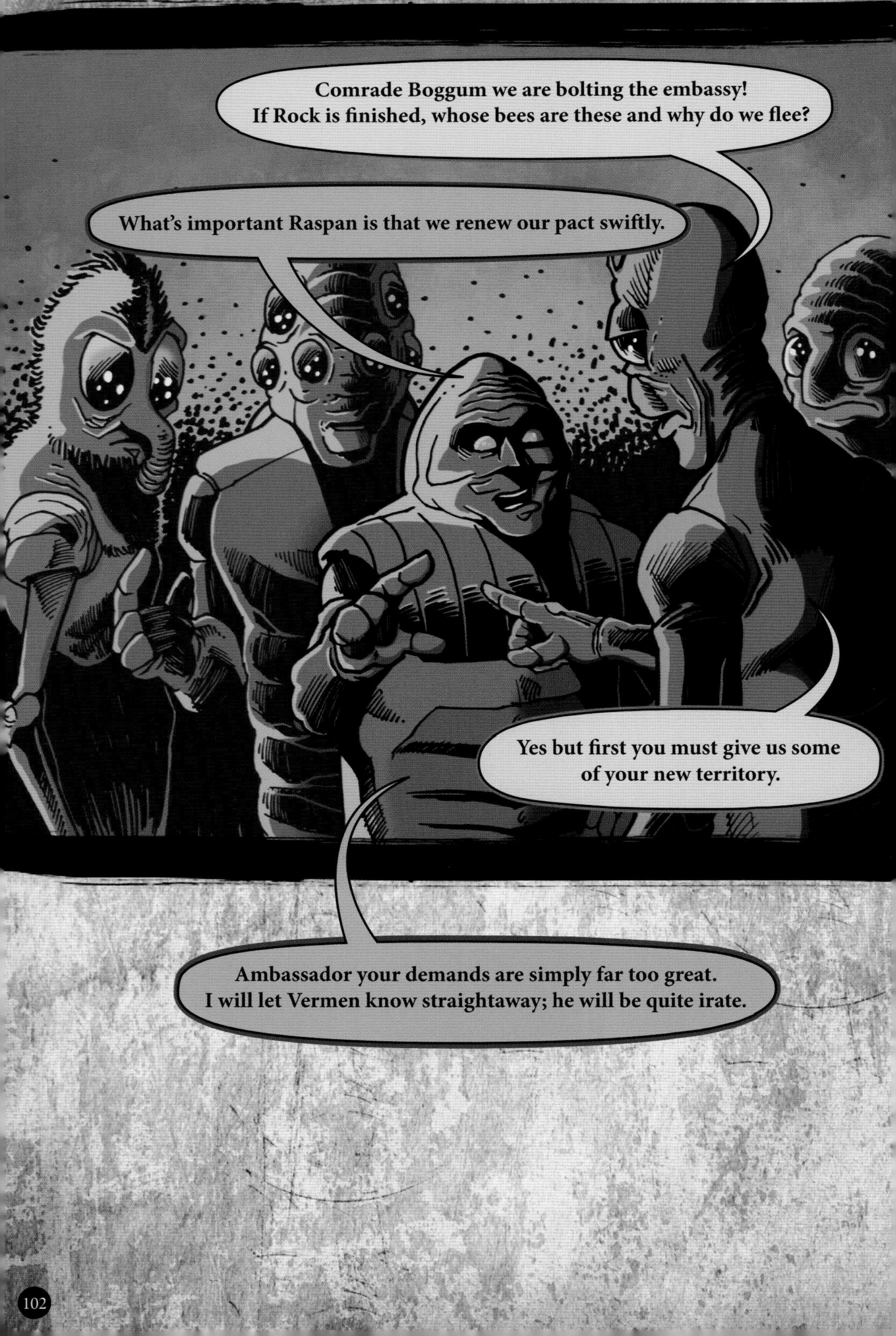
Comrade Boggum we are bolting the embassy!
If Rock is finished, whose bees are these and why do we flee?
What's important Raspan is that we renew our pact swiftly.
Yes but first you must give us some
of your new territory.
Ambassador your demands are simply far too great.
I will let Vermen know straightaway; he will be quite irate.

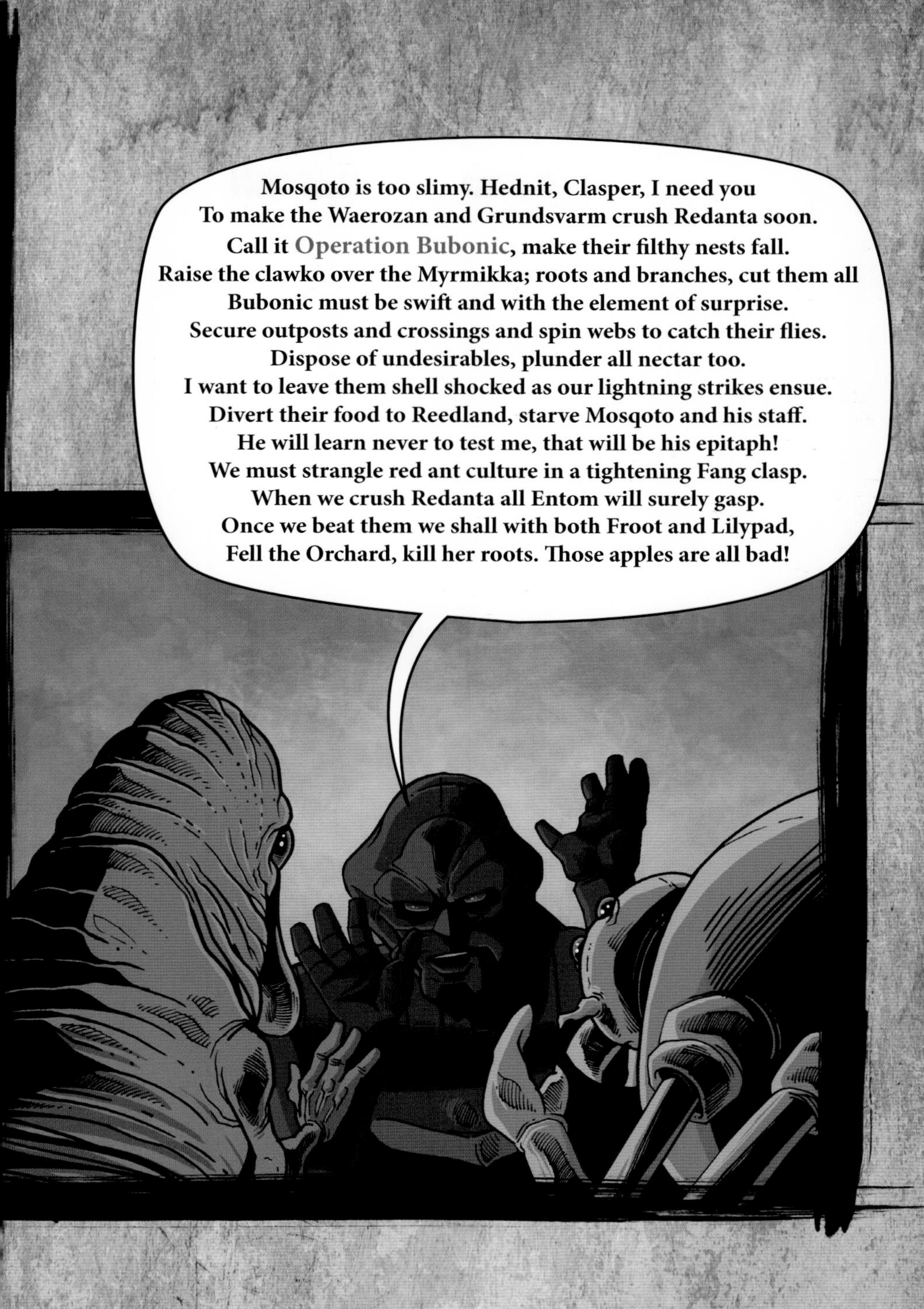
Mosqoto is too slimy. Hednit, Clasper, I need you
To make the Waerozan and Grundsvarm crush Redanta soon.
Call it Operation Bubonic, make their filthy nests fall.
Raise the clawko over the Myrmikka; roots and branches, cut them all
Bubonic must be swift and with the element of surprise.
Secure outposts and crossings and spin webs to catch their flies.
Dispose of undesirables, plunder all nectar too.
I want to leave them shell shocked as our lightning strikes ensue.
Divert their food to Reedland, starve Mosqoto and his staff.
He will learn never to test me, that will be his epitaph!
We must strangle red ant culture in a tightening Fang clasp.
When we crush Redanta all Entom will surely gasp.
Once we beat them we shall with both Froot and Lilypad,
Fell the Orchard, kill her roots. Those apples are all bad!

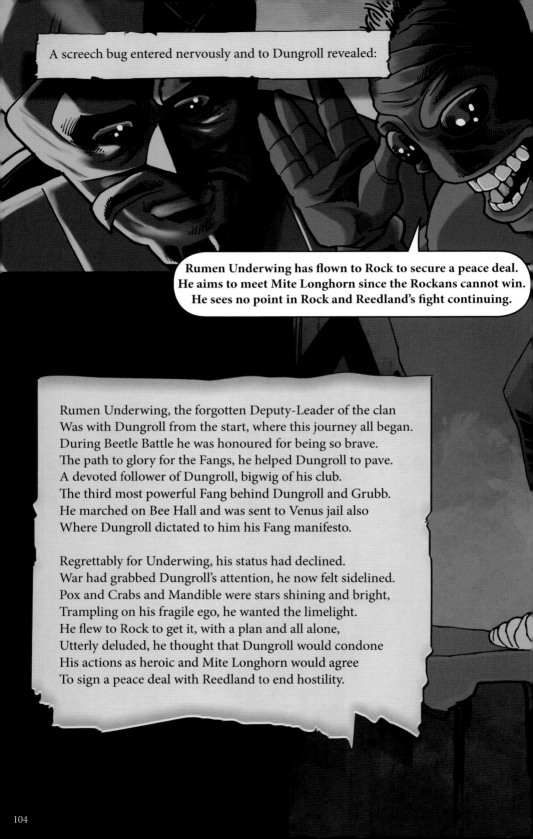

A screech bug entered nervously and to Dungroll revealed:

Rumen Underwing has flown to Rock to secure a peace deal.
He aims to meet Mite Longhorn since the Rockans cannot win.
He sees no point in Rock and Reedland's fight continuing.

Rumen Underwing, the forgotten Deputy-Leader of the clan
Was with Dungroll from the start, where this journey all began.
During Beetle Battle he was honoured for being so brave.
The path to glory for the Fangs, he helped Dungroll to pave.
A devoted follower of Dungroll, bigwig of his club.
The third most powerful Fang behind Dungroll and Grubb.
He marched on Bee Hall and was sent to Venus jail also
Where Dungroll dictated to him his Fang manifesto.

Regrettably for Underwing, his status had declined.
War had grabbed Dungroll's attention, he now felt sidelined.
Pox and Crabs and Mandible were stars shining and bright,
Trampling on his fragile ego, he wanted the limelight.
He flew to Rock to get it, with a plan and all alone,
Utterly deluded, he thought that Dungroll would condone
His actions as heroic and Mite Longhorn would agree
To sign a peace deal with Reedland to end hostility.

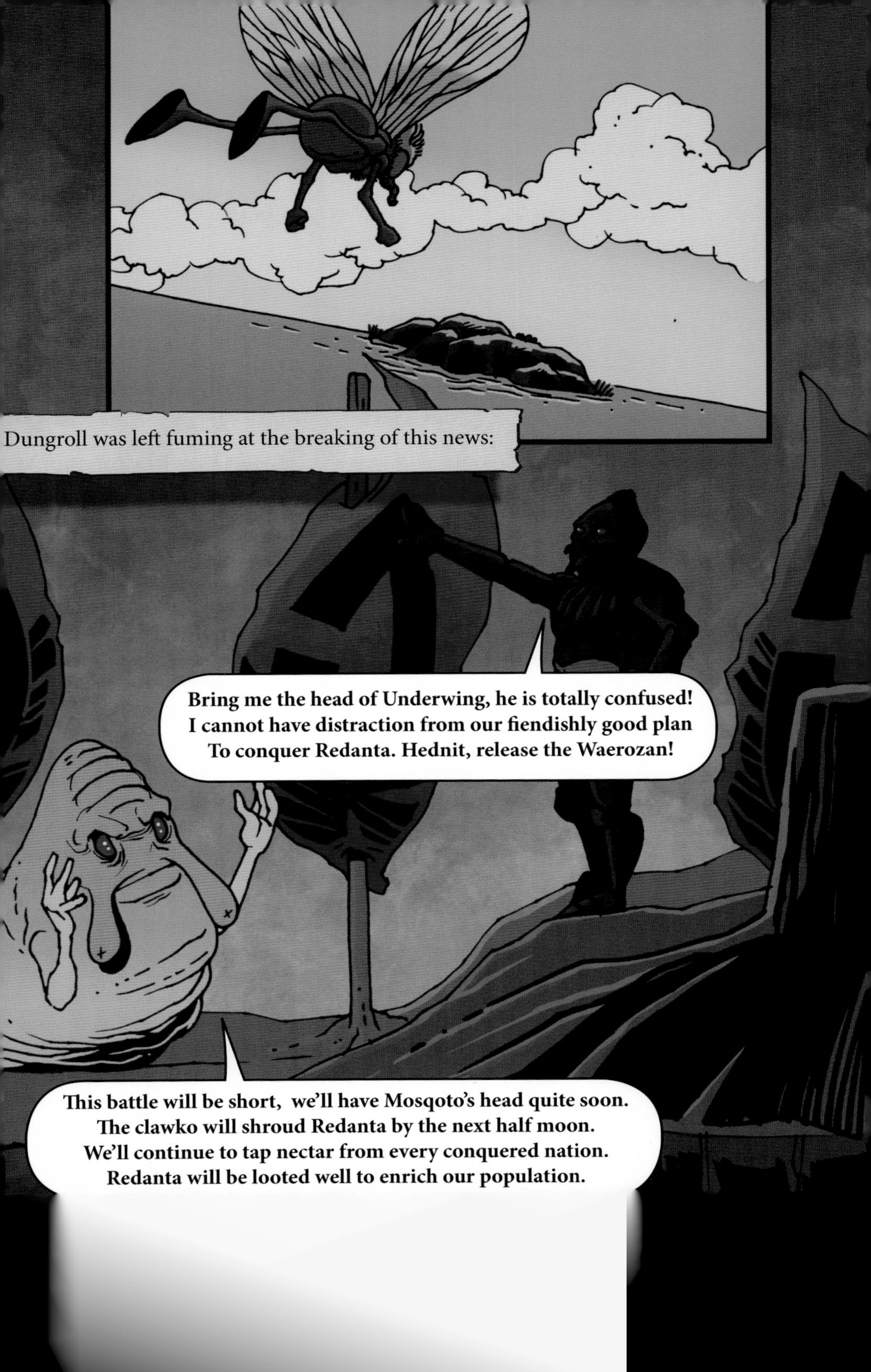
Dungroll was left fuming at the breaking of this news:
Bring me the head of Underwing, he is totally confused! I cannot have distraction from our fiendishly good plan To conquer Redanta. Hednit, release the Waerozan!
This battle will be short, we'll have Mosqoto's head quite soon. The clawko will shroud Redanta by the next half moon. We'll continue to tap nectar from every conquered nation. Redanta will be looted well to enrich our population.

Operation Bubonic began promptly and great inroads were made.
The Waerozan and Grundsvarm on their victory parade.
Both headed straight for Bivouac, Redanta's capital city,
Invading in tandem to cause the red ants misery.

The crushing of the Red forces soon turned into a rout.
A result of the purges that Mosqoto had carried out.
Poyson Mandible then screeched to all:

Redanta has attacked!
Reedland is defending and
Sending the critters back.

Mosqoto did not wish to provoke Dungroll in this war
So reports of Reedland's invasion he chose to just ignore.
The red ants retreated, devouring all plants as they went:
Denying the Reedans food as their energy was spent.
This lack of food for the Grundsvarm and for the Waerozan
Saw tiredness and absence rise, fractures in Dungroll's plan.
As they advanced, the Grundsvarm rounded up Red ladybirds
For slaughter in great numbers, they were heeding Dungroll's words.
Red prisoners of war were kept in termite mounds unfed
Then used for scientific tests, poisoned and left for dead.

Reports reached Mosqoto of the extent of Reedland's attack.
It dawned on him that this was real, he was taken aback.

If that dung beetle thinks that he can conquer our nation,
He is wrong, we'll give him his war of annihilation!

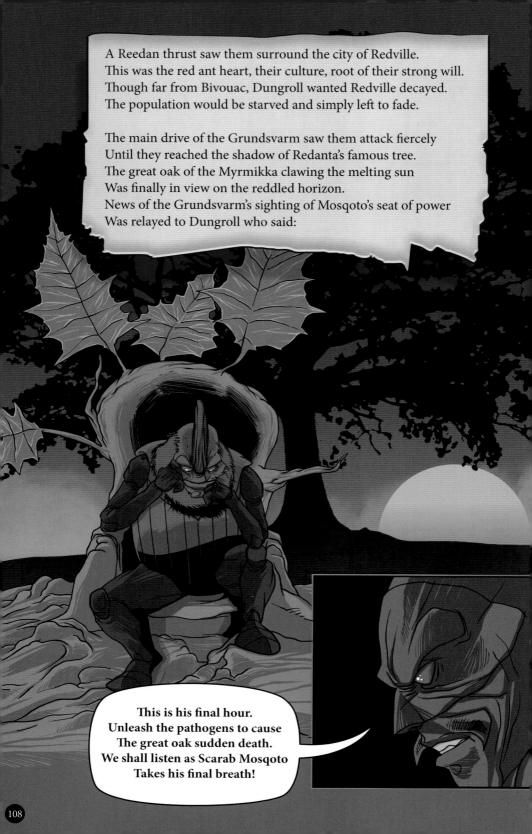

A Reedan thrust saw them surround the city of Redville.
This was the red ant heart, their culture, root of their strong will.
Though far from Bivouac, Dungroll wanted Redville decayed.
The population would be starved and simply left to fade.

The main drive of the Grundsvarm saw them attack fiercely
Until they reached the shadow of Redanta's famous tree.
The great oak of the Myrmikka clawing the melting sun
Was finally in view on the reddled horizon.
News of the Grundsvarm's sighting of Mosqoto's seat of power
Was relayed to Dungroll who said:

This is his final hour.
Unleash the pathogens to cause
The great oak sudden death.
We shall listen as Scarab Mosqoto
Takes his final breath!

Chapter 5
The Turning of the Worm

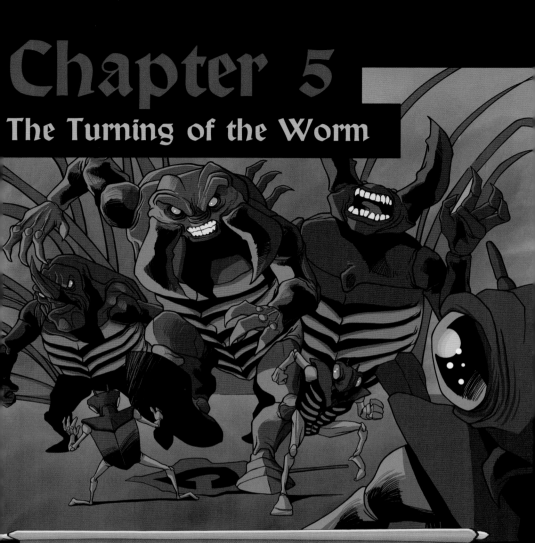

While Dungroll planned his victory speech, Mosqoto's troops fought back;
Driving the Reedans from Myrmikka and out of Bivouac.
The red ants kept reforming, more forces kept appearing,
Now came the great counter-attack that the Reedans had been fearing.
The Reedans had inflicted on the Reds much injury
But now they faced a backlash which was borne of pure fury.

Red ant monsters now emerged of great strength, speed and size.
Goliath stag beetles appeared before shocked Reedan eyes.
Bites did not harm this titan and stings bounced off its shell too.
There seemed little that the Grundsvarm or the Waerozan could do.
It attacked without due mercy and quickened Reedland's retreat.
Making a mockery of Dungroll's battlefield elite.

Dungroll ordered:

Hold your positions, do not take one step back.
If you flee you will be executed by the swift mantis attack!

Leading the drive against Reedland was General Coleo,
A clever, strategic soldier admired by Mosqoto.
He was decorated for bravery in Beetle Battle and
Had fought in Redanta's civil war before joining the red ant clan.
In the Manor Farm war, two seasons before at Redanta's farthest border
He ensnared and killed a Lilypad swarm of snipers and marauders.
Now here he was beating the Waerozan and Grundsvarm too,
Causing Dungroll to rage, take breath and then to rage anew.

You Generals have no shell, you're soft. I shall command instead.
Anyone who retreats, I repeat, will surely end up dead!

This order was ignored by countless tired Grundsvarm who
Went absent without leave, retreated or vanished from view.

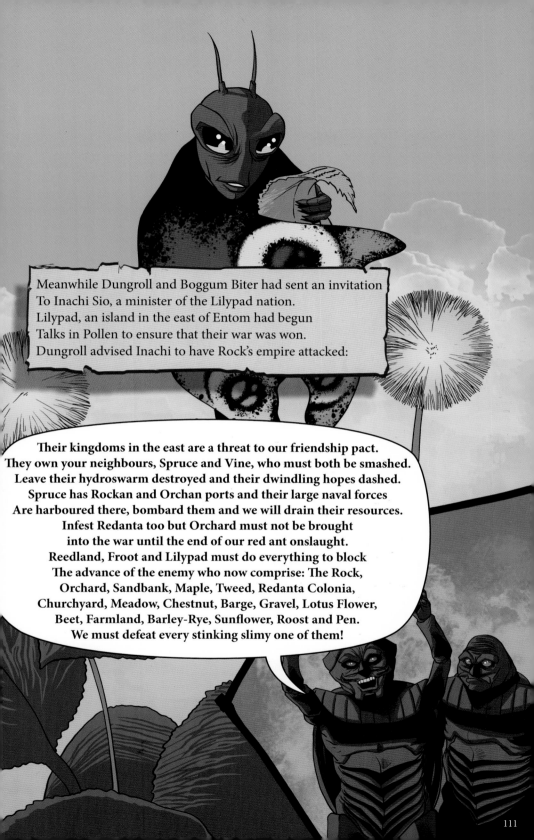

Meanwhile Dungroll and Boggum Biter had sent an invitation
To Inachi Sio, a minister of the Lilypad nation.
Lilypad, an island in the east of Entom had begun
Talks in Pollen to ensure that their war was won.
Dungroll advised Inachi to have Rock's empire attacked:

Their kingdoms in the east are a threat to our friendship pact.
They own your neighbours, Spruce and Vine, who must both be smashed.
Leave their hydroswarm destroyed and their dwindling hopes dashed.
Spruce has Rockan and Orchan ports and their large naval forces
Are harboured there, bombard them and we will drain their resources.
Infest Redanta too but Orchard must not be brought
into the war until the end of our red ant onslaught.
Reedland, Froot and Lilypad must do everything to block
The advance of the enemy who now comprise: The Rock,
Orchard, Sandbank, Maple, Tweed, Redanta Colonia,
Churchyard, Meadow, Chestnut, Barge, Gravel, Lotus Flower,
Beet, Farmland, Barley-Rye, Sunflower, Roost and Pen.
We must defeat every stinking slimy one of them!

Dungroll was not told of Lilypad's other idea,
They had entered peace talks in the Orchard's capital, Buddleia.
Despite these talks both with Reedland and with the Orchard too,
Lilypad launched a surprise attack on Orchard's fleet and crew.
The target, Willow Waterbase, a busy Orchan dock
With waterbugs of every kind replenishing their stock.
In vast numbers the Orchans gathered at this island quay
And were slaughtered in a morning raid by their enemy.

Orchans were shocked, Entom was shocked, Dungroll was shocked too.
For him it was bad timing by Lilypad's hasty crew.
His Grundsvarm was fighting the Reds, he simply did not need
The Orchard entering the fray with her huge swarms rallied.

The Orchans had a large terrain to Entom's farthest west
Comprised of many colonies, some gained by sharp conquest.
It was once part of Rock's empire but wrenched free long ago
And during Beetle Battle helped to slay the Reedan foe.
Once Reedland had invaded Meadow, causing war again,
The Orchard sent supplies to Rock to aid her war campaign.
The Orchan threat was something that Dungroll could not ignore
So he announced:

AGAINST THE ORCHARD, REEDLAND DECLARES WAR!

Meanwhile on Farmland's field which lay north-west of Barley-Rye
Stood the nation of Grayn with hills of seeds reaching high.
Both Rock and Reedland had troops in Grayn and they now did brawl
To end each other's epic rise and spark a brutal fall.
Commanding Reedland's Farmland force was General Vulpine,
He had helped smash Sandbank's defence and advance Reedland's frontline.
His nemesis in Farmland was Rock's General Cinnabar
Who had served in Beetle Battle and was a strategic star.

This classic clash saw both sides gain then lose the upper hand
But in the end Rock triumphed, driving Reedland from Farmland.
Reedland's loss was hastened by Dungroll under-supplying
General Vulpine's troops with food, their campaign ended up dying.
Also Rock and Orchard had swarms based nearby in Malt
And from there they launched against Vulpine's troops their joint assault.
Rock had recruited volunteers from her vast kingdom and
Sent them to fight far from their homes to meet her war demands.

Those from Farmland for example had instructions to repel
Lilypad's advance to Lotus Flower; they fought well.
On mountains and in thickets side by side with Rock's elite,
Farmland's young bugs battled through the downpours, mud and heat.
Those from Lotus Flower, Roost, Maple, Spruce, Vine and Pen,
As they did in Beetle Battle, formed units once again.
These troops of Rock's realm, overlooked by history
Gave their lives to Rock's struggle and the fight for liberty.

In Redanta meantime things were also *not* going to plan;
Mosqoto's fliers had rid all trace of the Waerozan.
The Grundsvarm was famished and they upon Dungroll's command
Entered Mosqoton City to pillage and feed off the land.
Mosqoton City was far from Redville and Bivouac,
Dungroll wanted it obliterated, erased from the map.
His reason was simple, it was named after Mosqoto
So crushing it would deal the Reds a devastating blow.
Beyond it also lay the flowerbeds of the Honey Field
Where the hungry swarms could feast on that rich nectar yield.

So did enter half of the entire Grundsvarm force.
Mosqoton was a diversion from their original course.
Supported by the Siafu, all had tasted victory
From Meadow through to Sandbank, now they fought for more glory.
The Reedan thrust began to fail, Redanta was too vast.
The Waerozan and Grundsvarm twin strikes were no longer fast.
Their communication had broken down, supplies had faltered too.
The red ants began to surround them, Reedland found no way through.

Reedland's General Urtica leading the Mosqoton attack
Saw the red snare forming and requested that the troops pull back.
Dungroll rejected this outright shrieking:

> **You must not retreat!**
> **Hold every position until your**
> **Mission is complete!**

By now the worm had turned and the mild weather had turned too,
A burst of hailstones covered Redanta and a tempest blew.

The frozen landscape stopped the Grundsvarm fighters in their tracks
Which allowed the red ants to launch swift counter-attacks.
Their swarm was well prepared, fought on bravely through the freeze
And their scorpion flies, snow flies and springtails trod the ice with ease.

The Grundsvarm razed Mosqoton but the red ants did not bend,
In fact the rubble's perfect cover helped them to defend.
Huge numbers of stag beetles joined the battle for the Reds,
Tightening the noose and leaving many Grundsvarm dead.
Throughout the city Reedland's General Urtica stopped the fight.
His ermine moth flapped overhead with wings both broad and white.
The battle of Mosqoton City died down and a silence
Reigned once again over this land, witness to much violence.

On the Pond Reedland's water scorpions wreaked havoc upon
Supply convoys to Rock trying to break through the cordon.
These four scorpions, fiercer than any Rockan bug
Were as stealthy as a stick insect and as quiet as a slug.
Mite Longhorn feared them for they sank Rock's hydroswarm at will,
Any Rockan vessel that peeped forth was seen, taken and killed.
The Rockan Air Force was ordered to hunt and destroy all.
Longhorn believed that if they failed, Entom would soon fall.
Locating the water scorpions was a difficult task indeed;
They ambushed quickly then vanished, hiding in pondweed.

Meanwhile the citizens of Redville had begun to starve,
The siege of their city had seen their population halve.
Carcasses lay everywhere, some were still alive.
Strange flesh was severed and eaten in order to survive.

In Reedland the Rockan Air Force was causing devastation,
Grasshopper raids devoured towns across the Reedan nation.
The Waerozan had shown the Rockans how to wreckz a city
And now the Rockans chose to pay them back without due pity.

Dungroll increased his plan for the mass insecticide
Of ladybirds and others whom he wanted 'purified'.
Redanta and Meadow were to have their cultures dissolved
And now he gave more detail of what that change involved.

The Meadow bugs will be our slaves, bugs from Churchyard too.
Ladybirds must be extinct, the mentally ill slew.
We are the sovereign creed and our fruits must be spread.
Males who will not reproduce might also end up dead.
Red ant workers shall toil for Reedland until they die.
Prisoners of war shall be fed a minimal supply.

Grundsvarm atrocities in conquered lands were commonplace.
Pox and Grimmstone had created special units just to trace
Ladybirds, red ants, Farmlanders, the disabled too
And massacre them in groups at a suitable venue.
The victims had to dig mass graves before they were all stung,
Whole colonies were wiped out from the old down to the young.

But this method of death was too messy and too slow.
What Grimmstone wanted was a way to kill more with one blow.
The solution required cramming crowds into a termite mound
With a chimney above the surface and a chamber underground.
Once in, the exits were all sealed and methanogen bacteria
Were released inside the chamber to poison the interior.
These microbes produced methane gas which suffocated all,
Leaving a heap of slain bodies at least a metre tall.
Other inmates of the termite mound were forced to haul the dead
And place them on a nearby sundew plant's sticky pinhead.
The enzymes of the plant dissolved the bodies rapidly,
Leaving no trace of the victims of this mass butchery.

Meanwhile an uprising took place by ladybirds in Meadow
Who had been starved, jammed together and forced to live in a ghetto.
They should have been dispatched by now yet managed to survive
Which irritated Grimmstone who did not want them alive.
They rebelled against the Fang guards who had tried to relocate
The lot of them to termite mounds and no doubt seal their fate.
Their brave resistance lasted days but ultimately failed
As the greater weapons of the Grundsvarm and WETA prevailed.
The Battle of Meadow's Ghetto tore the region down,
The ladybird population cleansed, the ghetto a ghost-town.

By now, the Fang medical tests mentioned earlier
Were using ladybirds and foes for mad science fodder.
Probes were done to view how long victims could endure
Great cold before death freed them from organ failure.
Other tests had worms sliced into sections just to see
How many segments could be made to reform naturally.

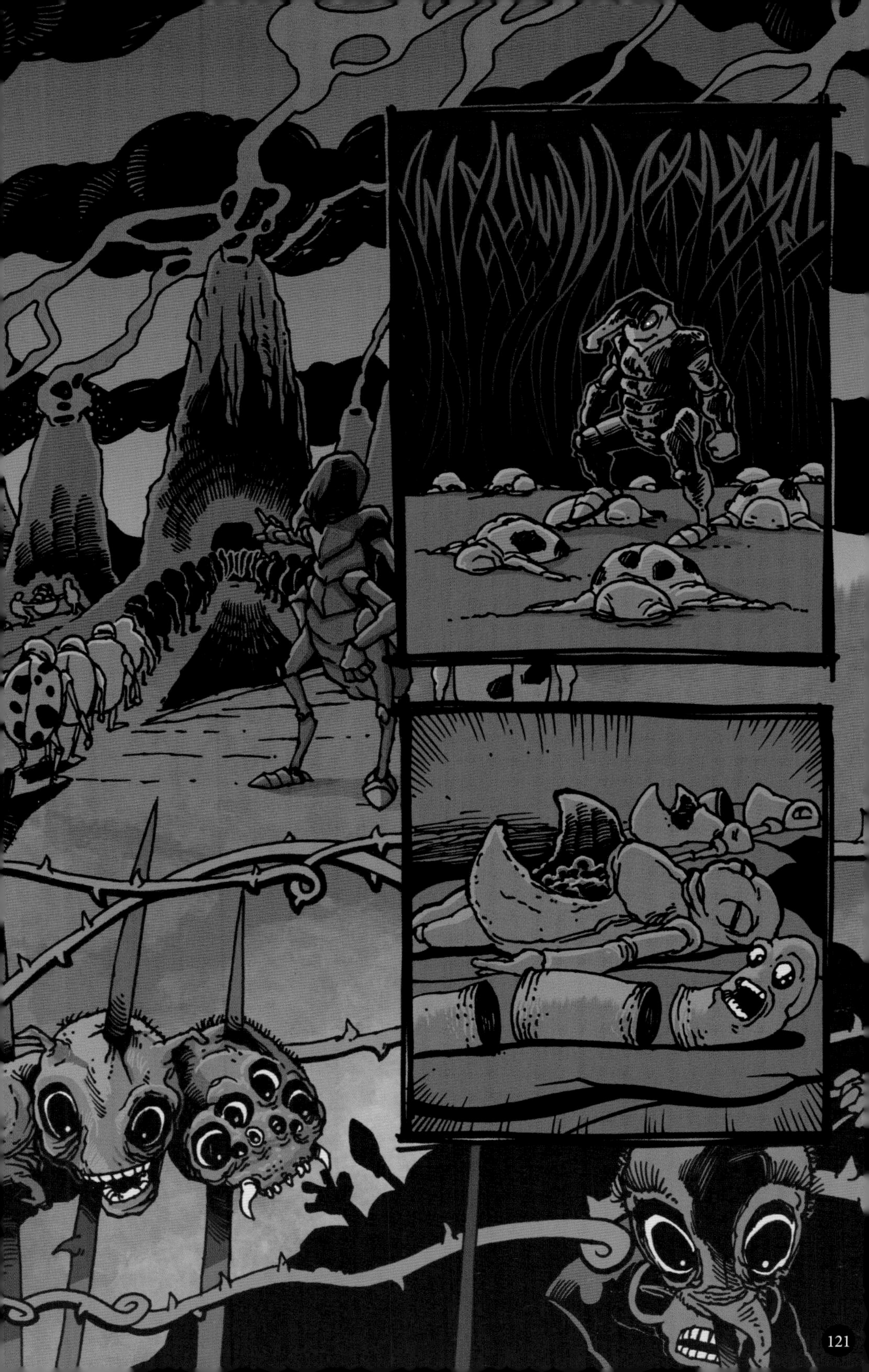

Resistance to the Fangs continued firmly in Churchyard.
A little group with help from Rock now planned to hit them hard.
They laid mines in a narrow pass aiming to nullify
Dungroll's favourite henchbug as his convoy scurried by.
The mines they used were antlions, a beast that lay in wait
Buried just beneath the surface, waiting to detonate.

The target was Grimmstone himself, now Churchyard's Dark-Lord
Whose ruthless ways impressed Dungroll, promotion his reward.
Proclaimed as the standard of the 'superior Fang breed',
His sights were high, his master Pox, he aimed to supersede.
His pseudonyms were manifold: The Deadly Caterpillar,
Pox's Evil Demon, The Beastly Yellow Killer,
The Slaughterer of Steeple,   The Executioner too.
The more he massacred, the more his reputation grew.

Grimmstone's cortège entered the pass and stopped for a quick preen.
His narrow, icy eyes darting around the sandy scene.
In glorious sunshine he basked with his wings ready to flap.
He then trotted a few steps forward and stepped onto a trap.

The antlion ignited, blasting forth its hollowed jaw
Which skewered Grimmstone quickly and dragged him through the floor.
A struggle took place underground, Grimmstone's three parts detached.
He was then liquidised and consumed in this stark mismatch.

The assassins fled to Underlog, a habitat nearby
And hid in the leaf litter to escape the Fang reply.
It was not long before Pox sent his odious delegation
To hunt the perpetrators of Grimmstone's assassination.
A trudging crescendo portended WETA drawing near.
It was the sound that instinctively everybody feared.
WETA encircled Underlog then tightened the snare,
Slaughtering the assassins plus two thousand who lived there.

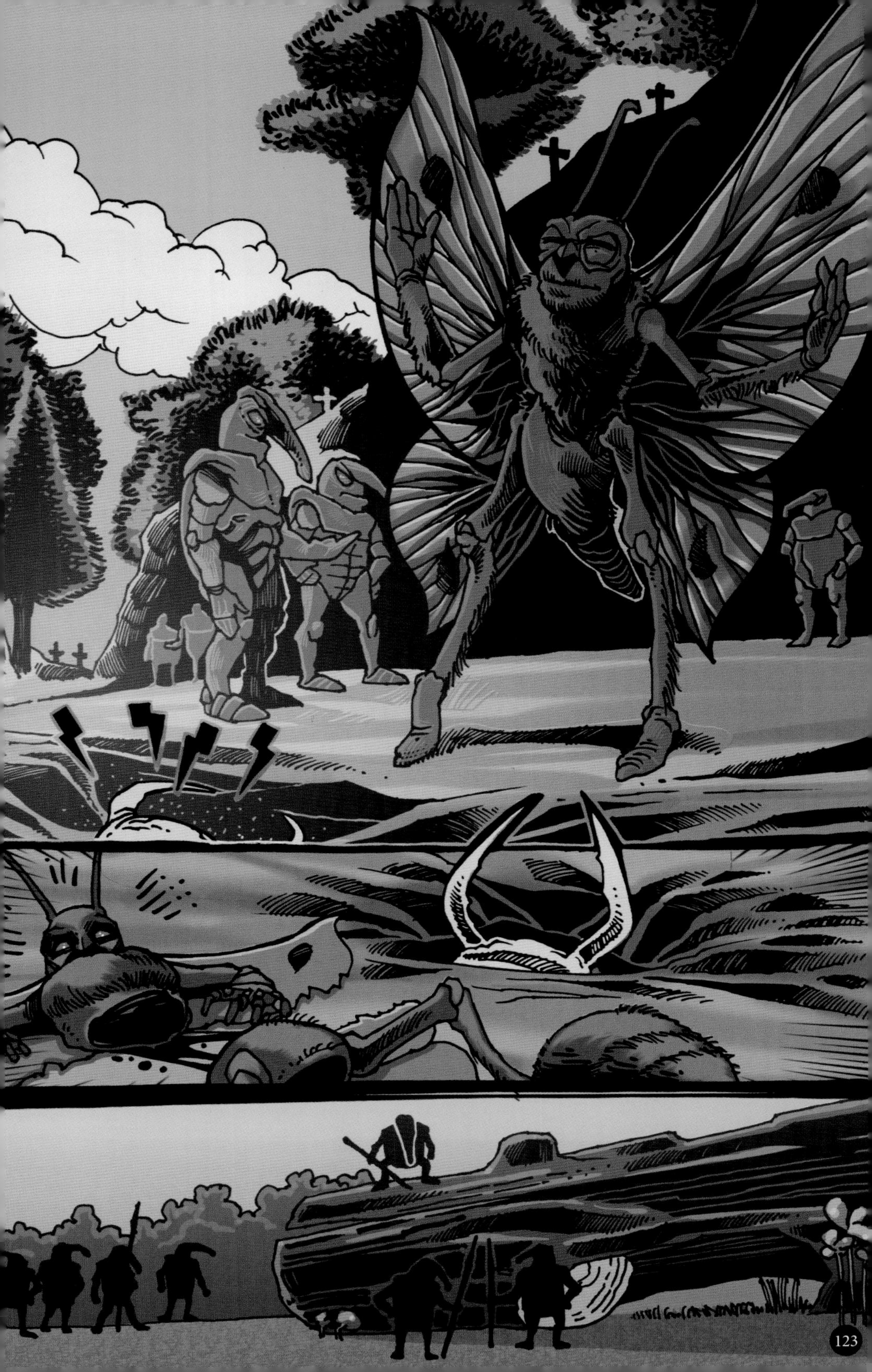

Bollwax Vanitis meantime had been summoned by his queen
To her hive in Froot to discuss the performance of his team.

Your relationship with Reedland and Lilypad is strong
But citizens of Froot have suffered as things have gone wrong.
The Orchard, Rock and their allies after freeing Farmland
Have fought their way to Toh, the island off our mainland!
I have no choice Vanitis, you are to be arrested
And stripped of all powers that I had previously vested.

Froot then announced its surrender; Dungroll was appalled.
Bollwax was jailed and an anti-Fang leader installed.

124

An event which had a great bearing on the war took place.
The stag beetles of Redanta battled face-to-face
Against the tiger beetles of the Grundsvarm's war machine
In the biggest armoured clash that Entom had ever seen.
The two sides ploughed into each other in a massive throw
Of the die by Vermen Dungroll and Scarab Mosqoto.

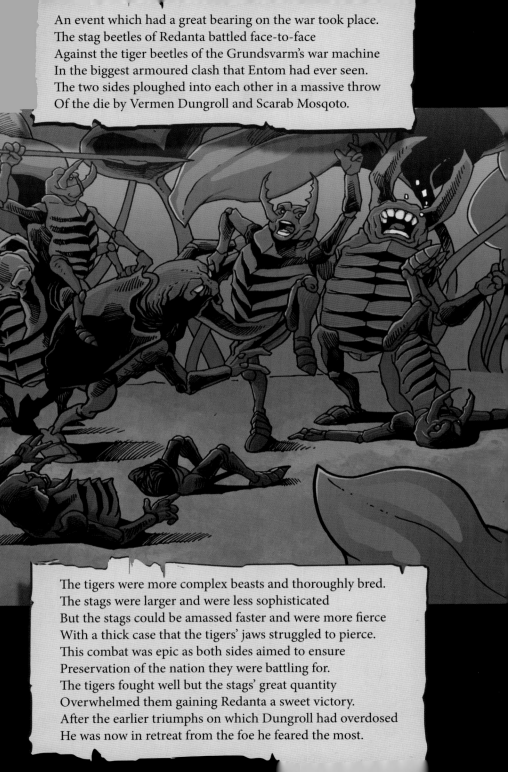

The tigers were more complex beasts and thoroughly bred.
The stags were larger and were less sophisticated
But the stags could be amassed faster and were more fierce
With a thick case that the tigers' jaws struggled to pierce.
This combat was epic as both sides aimed to ensure
Preservation of the nation they were battling for.
The tigers fought well but the stags' great quantity
Overwhelmed them gaining Redanta a sweet victory.
After the earlier triumphs on which Dungroll had overdosed
He was now in retreat from the foe he feared the most.

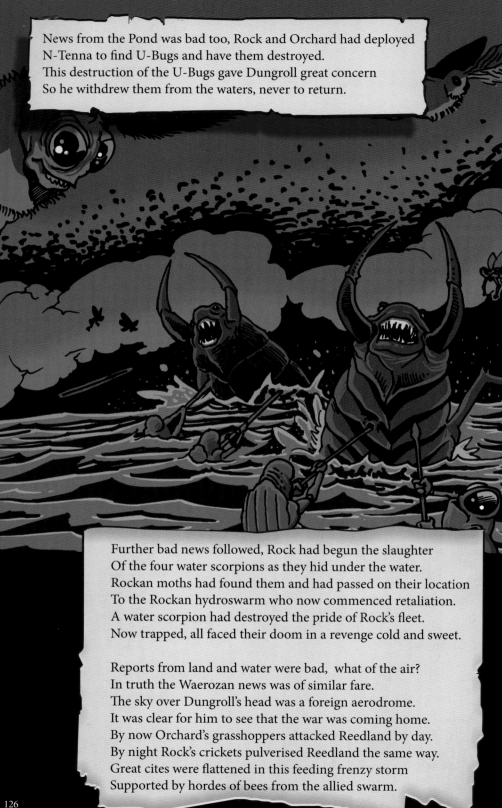

News from the Pond was bad too, Rock and Orchard had deployed
N-Tenna to find U-Bugs and have them destroyed.
This destruction of the U-Bugs gave Dungroll great concern
So he withdrew them from the waters, never to return.

Further bad news followed, Rock had begun the slaughter
Of the four water scorpions as they hid under the water.
Rockan moths had found them and had passed on their location
To the Rockan hydroswarm who now commenced retaliation.
A water scorpion had destroyed the pride of Rock's fleet.
Now trapped, all faced their doom in a revenge cold and sweet.

Reports from land and water were bad, what of the air?
In truth the Waerozan news was of similar fare.
The sky over Dungroll's head was a foreign aerodrome.
It was clear for him to see that the war was coming home.
By now Orchard's grasshoppers attacked Reedland by day.
By night Rock's crickets pulverised Reedland the same way.
Great cites were flattened in this feeding frenzy storm
Supported by hordes of bees from the allied swarm.

Part of that allied swarm was Squadron G,
Led by Orchard's charismatic Commander Cherry.
His team were bumblebees with distinctive red tails.
It was not just over Dungroll whom they had to prevail.
In the air they were free but on the ground on which they trod,
Other battles lay ahead for heroes of the G Squad.

Dungroll now reviewed his defence strategy.

A war on two fronts would be a calamity!
On the eastern front the red ants force us back;
On the western front the rest plan to attack.
We just cannot allow them to gain a foothold.
Increase the defence of Sandbank's beaches tenfold!
Our foes mass in Rock and from there they will attack
Across the Pond and into Sandbank; hold them back!
We must be ready for them, they must not get ashore.
The Pond must be their watery grave for evermore!

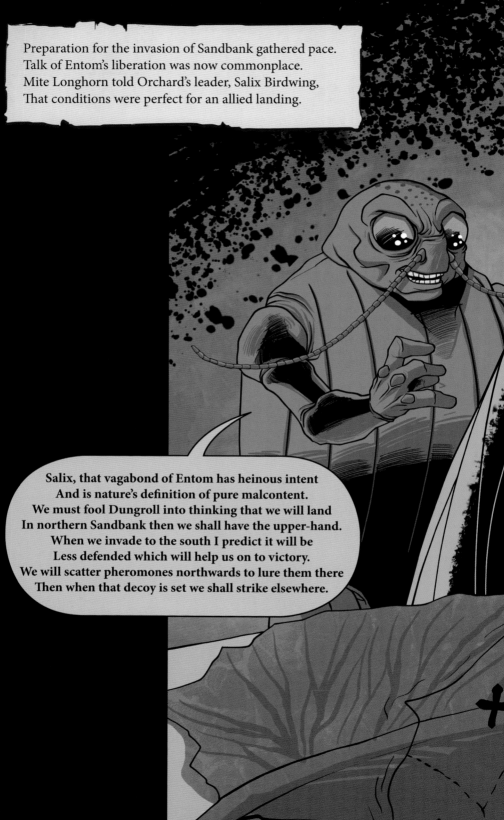

Preparation for the invasion of Sandbank gathered pace.
Talk of Entom's liberation was now commonplace.
Mite Longhorn told Orchard's leader, Salix Birdwing,
That conditions were perfect for an allied landing.

Salix, that vagabond of Entom has heinous intent
And is nature's definition of pure malcontent.
We must fool Dungroll into thinking that we will land
In northern Sandbank then we shall have the upper-hand.
When we invade to the south I predict it will be
Less defended which will help us on to victory.
We will scatter pheromones northwards to lure them there
Then when that decoy is set we shall strike elsewhere.

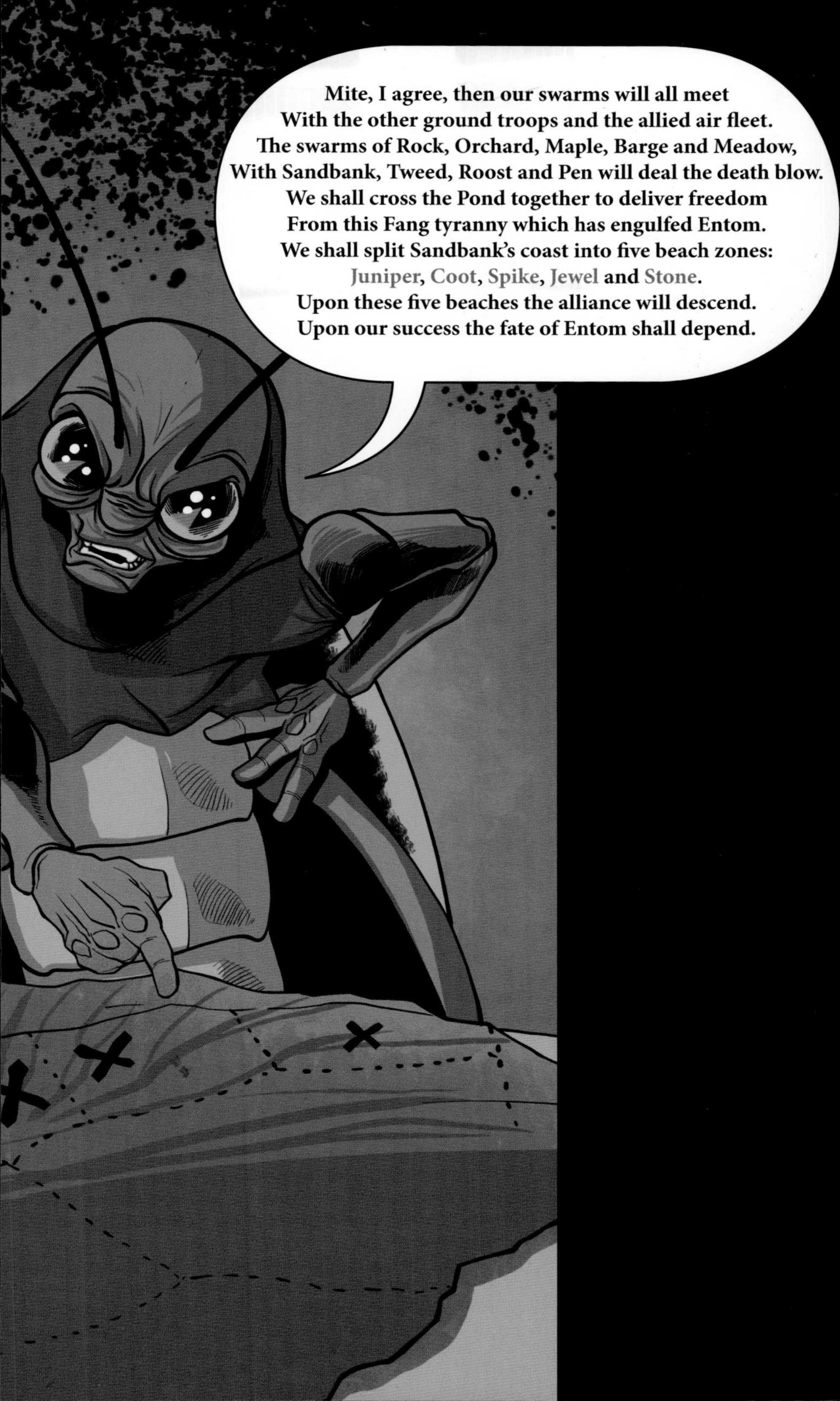
Mite, I agree, then our swarms will all meet
With the other ground troops and the allied air fleet.
The swarms of Rock, Orchard, Maple, Barge and Meadow,
With Sandbank, Tweed, Roost and Pen will deal the death blow.
We shall cross the Pond together to deliver freedom
From this Fang tyranny which has engulfed Entom.
We shall split Sandbank's coast into five beach zones:
Juniper, Coot, Spike, Jewel and Stone.
Upon these five beaches the alliance will descend.
Upon our success the fate of Entom shall depend.

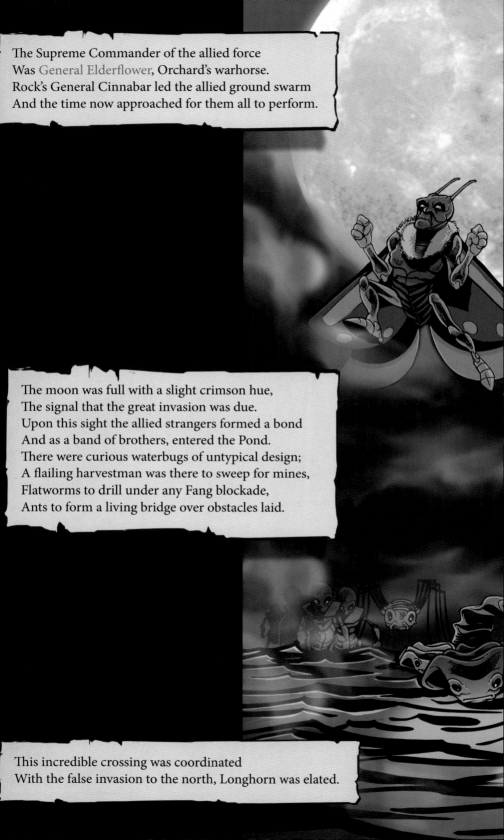

The Supreme Commander of the allied force
Was General Elderflower, Orchard's warhorse.
Rock's General Cinnabar led the allied ground swarm
And the time now approached for them all to perform.

The moon was full with a slight crimson hue,
The signal that the great invasion was due.
Upon this sight the allied strangers formed a bond
And as a band of brothers, entered the Pond.
There were curious waterbugs of untypical design;
A flailing harvestman was there to sweep for mines,
Flatworms to drill under any Fang blockade,
Ants to form a living bridge over obstacles laid.

This incredible crossing was coordinated
With the false invasion to the north, Longhorn was elated.

This decoy plan fooled the Fangs, it was a splendid trick.
Dungroll said:

They will attack the north, that is their tactic.
There their scent is strong so we must defend it well.
Move more troops to northern Sandbank! Follow their smell.

Although troops were moved northwards, thousands did remain
Along the entire coast to thwart the pending campaign.
Meanwhile Dungroll relaxed since the weather was poor:

They cannot cross a windswept Pond, that's for sure!

At that moment Rock's waterbug artillery fired,
Pounding the Reedan frontline heavily as required.
The first salvo released, the next bombardment was immense
As two hundred thousand allied troops attacked the Fang defence.
Armoured water snails ferried these forces across.
The Fangs attacked these water snails, inflicting severe loss.

With so many insects in one place, both sides were now susceptible
And were gnawed by knots of newts who found the whole thing highly edible.
Spiderlings from Sandbank, Rock and Maple parachuted
On to Spike, Jewel and Juniper beaches; many were executed.
The Orchans stormed Coot and Stone where resistance was severe,
Leaving swarms of them slain by the Reedan sharp frontier.
The Grundsvarm dug in on the beaches and the hills nearby,
Making a zone for allied troops to enter first, then die.

General Vulpine led the Fang beach defence strategy
Which was questioned and altered by Dungroll constantly.
With corpses on the beaches and floating in the water,
The Pond was a scene of apocalypse and slaughter.
Thousands lost their lives but the allies got ashore,
Gaining grips on beaches which they managed to secure.

Disembarked, the liberators battled into Sandbank's heart
Under fire from Reedans aiming to tear them apart.
The Waerozan's great damselflies were now in some distress
But the Grundsvarm's defence stunted the allied progress.
The heavy air attacks by allied bees enhanced
Their ground swarm and together the allies advanced.

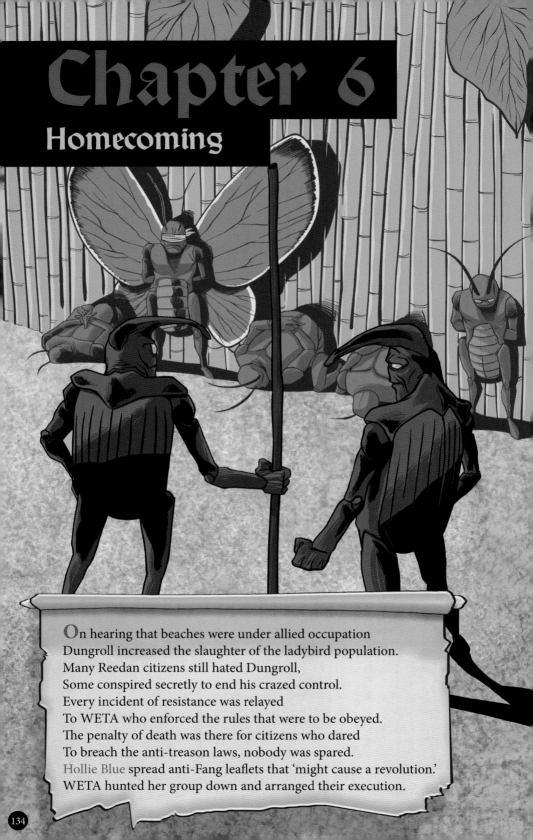

Chapter 6
Homecoming

On hearing that beaches were under allied occupation
Dungroll increased the slaughter of the ladybird population.
Many Reedan citizens still hated Dungroll,
Some conspired secretly to end his crazed control.
Every incident of resistance was relayed
To WETA who enforced the rules that were to be obeyed.
The penalty of death was there for citizens who dared
To breach the anti-treason laws, nobody was spared.
Hollie Blue spread anti-Fang leaflets that 'might cause a revolution.'
WETA hunted her group down and arranged their execution.

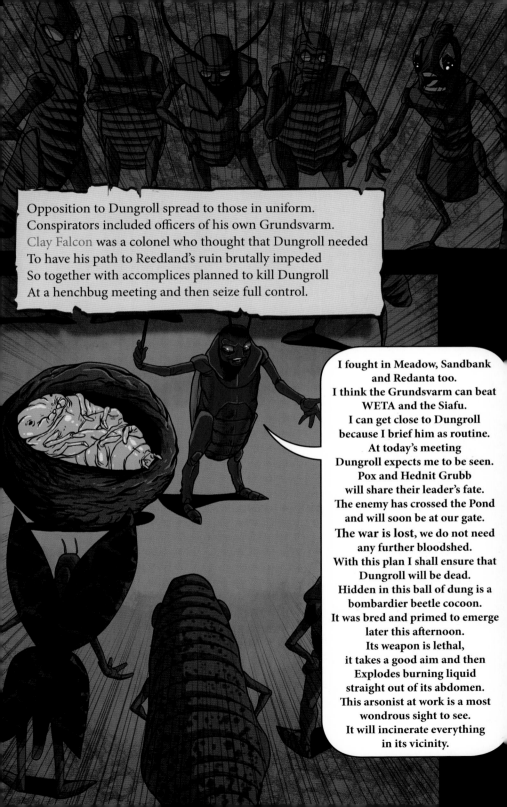

Opposition to Dungroll spread to those in uniform.
Conspirators included officers of his own Grundsvarm.
Clay Falcon was a colonel who thought that Dungroll needed
To have his path to Reedland's ruin brutally impeded
So together with accomplices planned to kill Dungroll
At a henchbug meeting and then seize full control.

I fought in Meadow, Sandbank
and Redanta too.
I think the Grundsvarm can beat
WETA and the Siafu.
I can get close to Dungroll
because I brief him as routine.
At today's meeting
Dungroll expects me to be seen.
Pox and Hednit Grubb
will share their leader's fate.
The enemy has crossed the Pond
and will soon be at our gate.
The war is lost, we do not need
any further bloodshed.
With this plan I shall ensure that
Dungroll will be dead.
Hidden in this ball of dung is a
bombardier beetle cocoon.
It was bred and primed to emerge
later this afternoon.
Its weapon is lethal,
it takes a good aim and then
Explodes burning liquid
straight out of its abdomen.
This arsonist at work is a most
wondrous sight to see.
It will incinerate everything
in its vicinity.

Clay took the ball and his journey to Dungroll's lair was swift.
When guards asked what the ball was for, he said:

It is a gift.

He placed the ball close to where Dungroll would normally sit
Then made his excuses and headed straight for the exit.
The meeting progressed as usual with Dungroll being briefed
On what his various Grundsvarms had recently achieved.
The henchbugs listened intently as each General in turn
Reported on the various battle lessons they had learned.

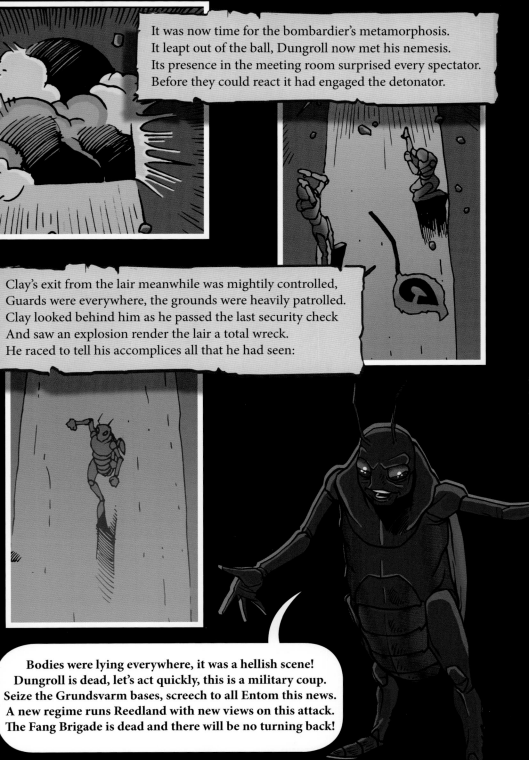

It was now time for the bombardier's metamorphosis.
It leapt out of the ball, Dungroll now met his nemesis.
Its presence in the meeting room surprised every spectator.
Before they could react it had engaged the detonator.

Clay's exit from the lair meanwhile was mightily controlled,
Guards were everywhere, the grounds were heavily patrolled.
Clay looked behind him as he passed the last security check
And saw an explosion render the lair a total wreck.
He raced to tell his accomplices all that he had seen:

Bodies were lying everywhere, it was a hellish scene!
Dungroll is dead, let's act quickly, this is a military coup.
Seize the Grundsvarm bases, screech to all Entom this news.
A new regime runs Reedland with new views on this attack.
The Fang Brigade is dead and there will be no turning back!

As the plotters left they got a terrible surprise.
Though injured and shaken, Dungroll had managed to survive.
By the hair on a bee's back, the coup amounted to a fail
And now Clay Falcon and his aides had WETA on their tail.
Pestilan Pox and WETA after a quick evaluation
Soon put Clay central to this attempted assassination.
Some in the lair were vaporised, murder was the indictment.
Now came the part Pox liked the most, the chase and the excitement.

You must hunt Clay down
And when you find him
Bring him here to me.
We will make an example
Of him and all who
Challenge our authority!

And so WETA sent wolf spiders to hunt their frightened prey.
Clay ran but he was found with very little delay.
He was snatched and brought to Pox where the grave charges were read
Then a mantis stepped forth to sever Clay's thorax from his head.
His accomplices were rounded up and endured a show-trial.
The guilty verdicts followed, their sentence was mantis-style.

Top Generals saw that they were now mistrusted by Dungroll.
He stripped many of power and gave himself field control.
General Vulpine, the nation's favourite, also had a fall.
The manner of it sent a stark message to one and all.
Injured in a Rockan bee attack and battling with poor health,
The heartless Dungroll ordered Vulpine to kill himself.
A Fang cortège arrived promptly at General Vulpine's nest.
A vial of spider venom was handed to him to ingest.
Bidding farewell to his kin he was marched out of the door
And ordered to gulp the contents. General Vulpine was no more.

Meantime the red ant ground swarm was rampaging in the east.
After clearing the Fangs from Fernland their confidence increased.
They hurtled through the nations of Rumyn and Boulder too,
Destination Reedland for an almighty rendezvous.
In the west, Sandbank was liberated, her capital Dune was free.
Sandbank resistance had severely disrupted Fang activity.
They routed their oppressors, killing some and harming more,
Causing the rest to retreat or face an allied encore.
Sandbank's General Corvid was their iconic mentor,
He had rejected all collaboration with the Fangs during the war.
Orchard's General Caddis urged the rampant ground swarms on:

Out of Sandbank, into Gravel, Aridland and beyond!

The Sanden and Gravellian ground swarms pushed on tirelessly
And with great help from Maple's beetles, Gravel was soon free.
Maple's swarm advanced to Froot to fight the Reedans there.
It was a tough, gutsy battle full of death and despair.

Dungroll needed more fighters on which he could depend
So larvae and the elderly were ordered to defend.

They were ill-equipped but to the rear-line they were forced to scramble.
It was in many ways for Dungroll a despairing gamble.

Desertion in the Grundsvarm peaked as they now bore the brunt
Of the allies, now in Reedland, storming on a wide front.
Reedland was running out of food, the Waerozan was hungry.
Flowerbeds had been lost, her hives produced less bees.
This meant that the Waerozan had little energy to fly
And were attacked on the ground as the allies ruled the sky.
But Dungroll was not done yet, he chose now to reveal
The next generation of fighters to get through this ordeal.
Bred in utmost secrecy at a site known to a few,
Dungroll's 'Terror Bugs' were ready to make their debut.

Some Terror Bugs are locusts
That fly quickly and then scour
The habitat below which they
Descend on and devour.
Other types are mongrels
Of both horsefly and botfly
Whose speed cannot be matched
And whose bite does terrify.
Those Terror Bugs fly faster than
Anything seen before.
When we launch them against Rock and Orchard
We will win this war.

They were duly launched against Pebble and other parts of Rock.
Devastating those neighbourhoods and leaving all in shock.
Fliers from Rock and Meadow stopped some locusts getting through
By knocking them off course, causing their attacks to miscue.
Halting the others required a different strategy,
Attacking them on the ground at the Terror Bug laboratory.

By now the allied thrust was of enormous magnitude.
Vast swathes of Reedland were occupied as the invaders continued
To scuttle towards Pollen causing Dungroll to retreat
To the sanctum of his lair to conjure wins from sure defeat.
Huge numbers of Grundsvarm surrendered, many were ensnared.
A route to Pollen opened but was heavily impaired.
The red ant General Coleo's ground swarm reached Pollen first,
Closely followed by Orchans once puddles were traversed.
The red ants arrived from the east, the Orchans from the west,
They met in the middle and celebrated their progress.

Target Dungroll! Where was he? It was their quest to find
The Fang leader and Second Beetle Battle's mastermind.

He was hiding in his lair with Poyson Mandible's family,
A few Siafu, Grundsvarm Generals and a clutch of devotees.
He looked awful, broken, shrunken, one leg twitched constantly.
He could hear the drone of allied wasps over his city.
So many henchbugs had deserted, Dungroll did not flee.
He hoped that his swarms would arrive like a cavalry.

Next thing, Dungroll was railing:

If we lose, Reedland will die!
This is unavoidable, only the fit survive!
Our best have been sacrificed, just the moult remains.
You let the enemy draw near and reverse all my gains!
My henchbugs have deserted me and I have been betrayed!

A screech bug entered nervously interrupting his tirade.

A message, sir, from Hednit Grubb: 'Vermen, our foes draw near.
I guess that you are cornered and cannot lead us from here.
If you are still in control then be sure to let me know.
The enemy must be repelled. Where is the death blow?
If I hear no reply from you by the closing of the flower,
I'll presume that you have lost command and will claim all of your power'

Dungroll slumped back, astonished, rocked to his very core
Then raged at the screech bug for bringing bad news to his door:

Guards, seize that messenger! Kill him for this humiliation.
That inept Hednit Grubb dares to give ME an ultimatum!

Before you do that sir, let me tell you a little more.
Pestilan Pox and the Orchans have conspired to end this war.
They aim to forge a committee of reconciliation
To draft a peace treaty between Reedland and Orchard's nation.

Dungroll respired audibly as if he was in pain.

This is the greatest treachery ever a bug sustained.
WETA must arrest Hednit, Chief Traitor to the end
But Pox's faithlessness wounds me; he and I were friends.

At that moment Boggum Biter entered Dungroll's lair.

Sir, the time has come for you to flee the allied snare.
Redanta's stag beetles have reached Pollen city centre.
The Orchans, in a race with them, have also swiftly entered.
They are mere moments away, this lair will be overrun
By red ants and Orchans before the setting of the sun.
What is more, Bollwax Vanitis has been murdered in Froot;
Stung by a crazed mob, hungry to execute.
His body publicly defiled and hanged in a town square.
This will not be your fate, I have made plans for your welfare.
A U-Bug waits to ferry you away from all of this
To a life of luxury and no victor's justice.

Dungroll smiled at Boggum, clasped him tenderly
And proceeded to explain to him why this cannot be.

If our reign is over and Reedland wilts and falls.
If the wide-ranging Fang empire melts with all who creep and crawl.
If our flights of fancy have been clipped of errant wings
And the six legs of the allies are better than our stings.
If we are to be stripped of all that we have achieved
Including lands conquered that many would have scarce believed,
Then Reedland shall be my grave. You go, this is your chance.
I stay to rally the Waerozan for Reedland's final stance!

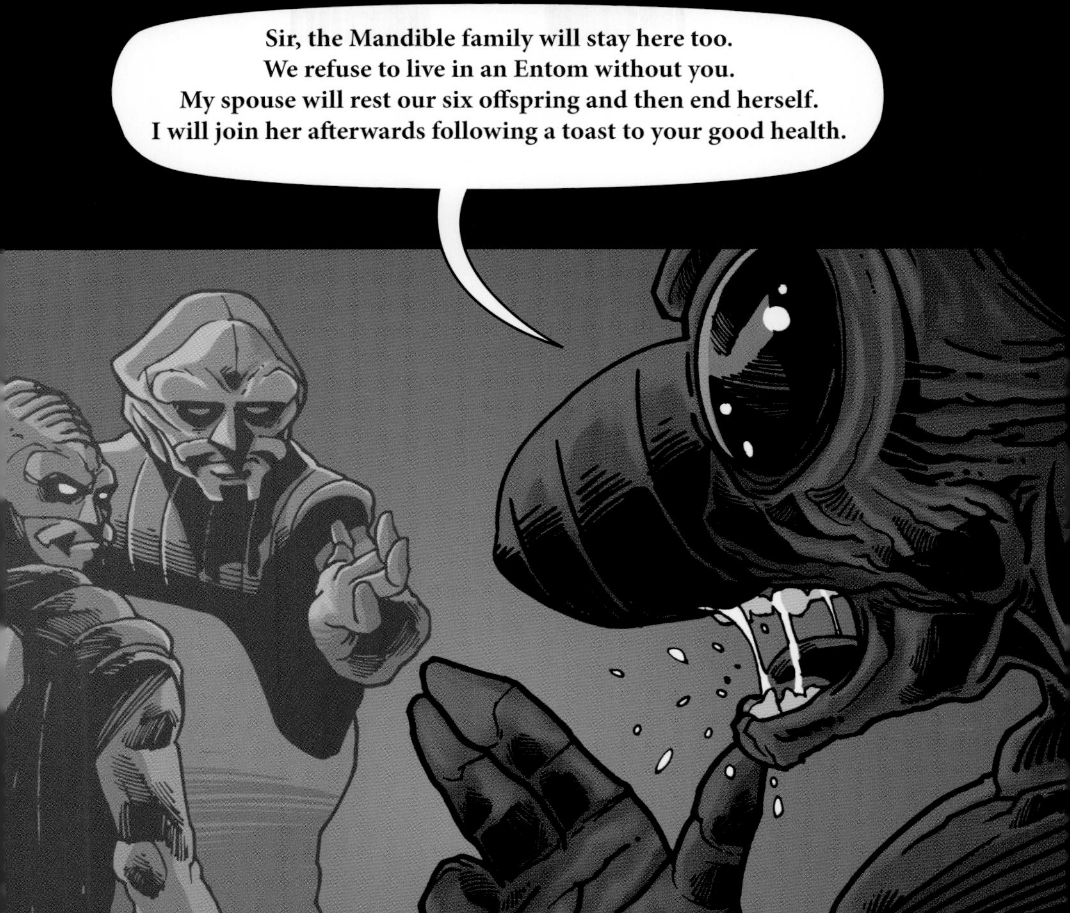
Sir, the Mandible family will stay here too.
We refuse to live in an Entom without you.
My spouse will rest our six offspring and then end herself.
I will join her afterwards following a toast to your good health.

As the end drew near Dungroll conceded to his fate.
He paired with a devotee, secretly courted, now his mate.
He then called Poyson aside to hear one final lament
And record his epitaph, his last will and testament.

The margin between victory and defeat is slender.
It is over Poyson, I choose death. I will not surrender!
Grubb and Pox have betrayed me. Grubb let the Waerozan down.
After I am gone Admiral Red must take my crown.
His hydroswarm fought valiantly and did not disappoint.
To be my successor, he is the one I shall anoint.
The Generals failed the Grundsvarm. The next Fang regime
Must continue to fight the ladybirds and their corrupt schemes.
When I am gone get enzymes and dissolve my whole body,
Lest I am shown in a flea circus as a curiosity.

All, everybody, please gather. My friends please do not grieve.
The time has finally arrived for me to take my leave.
I bid you farewell everyone, make haste, you are all free.
Escape the red ant trap, you are relieved of your duty.
I go to dine with the great Reedans at the ancient table.
The rise of the Fang Brigade will be Entom's greatest fable.

For his final act of the drama Dungroll retired to his nook.
His future at that moment had a very bleak outlook.
The nook was a small chamber at the rear of the lair.
He was accompanied by his bride, they were a wretched pair.
He had now disappeared from the observers' field of view.
They all waited silently, listening for a clue.
A long period passed and then they heard a thump.
They waited, peered into the nook and found the duo slumped.
An incredible sight! Dungroll, murderous architect of the war
With an empty vial of venom beside him on the floor.

Two burly guards strode forward, hauled the bodies out of the lair
And wrapped them in a silken web with the utmost of care.
The bodies were then placed into a ditch full of worms,
Maggots, parasites and decomposing germs.
This sickening bowl of scavengers consumed rapidly
Dungroll's carcass 'til there was nothing left to see.

Chapter 7
Final Sentence

As Dungroll was dissolving, Poyson gave his tribute.
Raising a claw for a final Fang Brigade salute.
He then sent a screech beetle to give Admiral Red the news.

Vermen is dead. You are in charge. The battle continues.

Poyson re-entered the lair, seeking his family.
His six grubs were all sleeping in the Mandible dormitory.
Together with his partner, prepared a special drink
And plunged beneath the lowest depth any parent could sink.
Into each mouth they dripped a drop which silenced every voice,
Killing their young with nightshade toxin, the poison of choice.
He then gave a Siafu soldier the chilling instruction
To kill him and his spouse and arrange their bodies' destruction.
The request was carried out and Poyson Mandible soon was dead;
Cleanly dispatched with the swift removal of his head.

As Boggum Biter had predicted, the lair was overrun
By rampant red ant fighters by the setting of the sun.
They found the bodies of Poyson, his mate and all their kin.
All other souls had fled as the red ants were approaching.

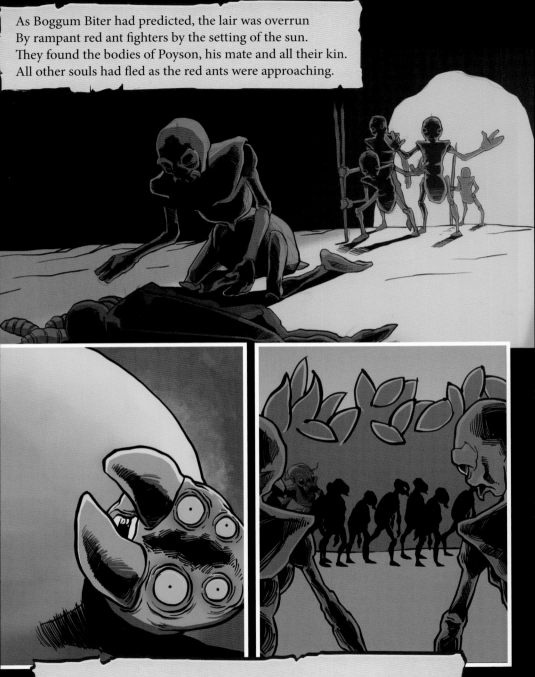

General Crabs was next to go, a self-inflicted end.
By now an allied victory was certainly the trend.
News was screeched through Reedland that Vermen Dungroll was dead.
The Grundsvarm fled the red ants, yielding to Orchans instead.

The Rockans spotted Pestilan Pox trying to get away,
Disguised as a ladybird, he was arrested the same day.
He knew that he faced trial, would lose and then be executed
So he chose to self-destruct before he could be prosecuted.

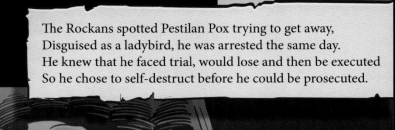

That was the end of Pox but others did face court in time,
Charged with mass insecticide and a host of other crimes.
The case of Hednit Grubb and two dozen others was heard.
Verdicts and sentences followed for crimes that had occurred.

Rumen Underwing: Guilty!
Sentenced to life in jail.
He was given credit for seeking peace
Although to no avail.

Boggum Biter: Guilty!
His sentence was death
For aiding war, consigning many
To their final breath.

Hednit Grubb: Guilty!
Sentenced to death too
But swallowed smuggled venom
To dodge the hangman's rendezvous.

From election campaigns and winning power, to dictator with full control,
To conquering of vast territories, to achieving the perverted goal.
From Stomp Squads to Terror Bugs, technologies were advanced.
An economy was repaired and a realm was enhanced.
From redefining warfare to mass extermination,
The depravity of the Fang Brigade affected every nation.
Millions died, cities were razed and empires were lost because
Beetles went to battle and what a battle it was!

GLOSSARY AND HISTORICAL REFERENCES

Admiral Red	Karl Dönitz, German admiral
Aridland	Austria
Barge	Norway
Barley-Rye	Abyssinia
Battle of Meadow's Ghetto	The Warsaw Ghetto Uprising
Bee Hall coup	Munich Beer Hall putsch
Beet	Mexico
Beetle Battle	World War 1
Biter	See Boggum Biter
Bivouac	Moscow
Bloodfire	See Raspan Bloodfire
Blu Mantid	Vasily Blokhin, Soviet executioner
Boggum Biter	Joachim von Ribbentrop, German foreign minister
Bollwax Vanitis	Benito Mussolini, Italian prime minister
Boulder	Bulgaria
Buddleia	Washington DC
Chestnut	Brazil
Churchyard	Czechoslovakia
Clasper Crabs	Hans Krebs, German general
Clawko	Swastika
Clay Falcon	Claus von Stauffenberg, German colonel
Commander Cherry	Benjamin O. Davis Jr, U.S. commander
Convolvulus Vormica	Kliment Voroshilov, Soviet commissar for defence
Coot	Utah beach, Normandy
Daisyland	Prussia
Dann De Leon	Édouard Daladier, French prime minister
Ducknest	Denmark
Dungroll	Adolf Hitler, German führer
Dungroll Grub Camps	Hitler Youth camps
Evergreen	Sweden
Fang/ Fang Brigade	Nazi Party
Farmland	Africa
Fernland	Finland
Filas Fungrus	Gregor Strasser, Nazi activist
Froot	Italy
Garden	The Sudentenland
General Caddis	George Patton, U.S. general
General Cinnabar	Bernard Montgomery, British field marshal
General Coleo	Georgy Zhukov, Soviet general

General Corvid	Charles de Gaulle, leader of Free France
General Elderflower	Dwight Eisenhower, U.S. general
General Urtica	Friedrich Paulus, German field marshal
General Vulpine	Erwin Rommel, German field marshal
Goliath stag beetle	Soviet T-34 tank
Grassland	Braunschweig state, Germany
Gravel	Belgium
Grayn	Egypt
Gräze	Warsaw
Grimmstone	Reinhard Heydrich, Nazi with many roles
Grubb	See Hednit Grubb
Grundsvarm	Panzers/ German armoured fighting vehicles
Hednit Grubb	Hermann Goering, German politician and leading Nazi
Hollie Blue	Sophie Scholl, German anti-Nazi activist
Honey Field	Oil fields of the Caucasus
Horsefly	Spitfire
Hydroswarm	Navy
Inachi Sio	Yosuke Matsuoka, Japanese foreign minister
Jewel	Gold beach, Normandy
Juniper	Juno beach, Normandy
Ladybirds	The Jewish community
Lasius Rabie	Lavrentiy Beria, Soviet chief of security
Leaf of honour	Munich Agreement
Lilypad Island	Japan
Limestone	Luxembourg
Longhorn	See Mite Longhorn
Lotus Flower	India
Lower Daffodil	Lippe, Germany
Maple	Canada
Meadow	Poland
Mite Longhorn	Winston Churchill, U.K. prime minister
Monarch	Kaiser Wilhelm II of Germany
Mosqoto	See Scarab Mosqoto
Mosqoton City	Stalingrad
Mulberry	Hungary
Myrmikka	The Kremlin
Nesterwing	See Spirac Nesterwing
Nettle	Ardennes forest, Belgium
Night of the Sharp Stings	The Night of the Long Knives
N-Tenna	Radar
Old Creek Bay	Coventry
Old Grey	Paul von Hindenburg, German president

Operation Bubonic	Operation Barbarossa/ Plan for German invasion of the Soviet Union
Operation Frog	Operation Sea lion/ Plan for German invasion of Great Britain
Operation Whitefly	Fall Weiss/ Plan for German invasion of Poland
Orchard	United States of America
Pebble	London
Pen	New Zealand
Pestilan Pox	Heinrich Himmler, leader of the SS
Pine	Alderney
Pollen	Berlin
Pond	The English Channel
Pox	See Pestilan Pox
Poyson Mandible	Joseph Goebbels, German minister of propaganda
Pride of Rock's fleet	HMS Hood
Raspan Bloodfire	Vyacheslav Molotov, Soviet foreign minister
Red ants	Communists
Red Mayfly	The Red Baron, Manfred von Richthofen
Redanta Colonia	Soviet Union
Redville	Leningrad
Reedland	Germany
Rock	Great Britain
Rockan Forum	House of Commons
Roost	Australia
Root Palace	German Reich chancellery building
Rumen Underwing	Rudolf Hess, German deputy führer
Rumyn	Romania
Salix Birdwing	Franklin D. Roosevelt, U.S. president
Sandbank	France
Scarab Mosqoto	Joseph Stalin, Soviet Union leader
Senate	The Reichstag/ German parliament building
Siafu	The SS / Schutzstaffel
Skyberry	Nuremberg
Spike	Sword beach, Normandy
Spirac Nesterwing	Neville Chamberlain, U.K. prime minister
Spruce	Singapore
Squadron G	The Tuskegee airmen
Steeple	Prague
Stik Pincer	Ernst Röhm, German SA chief of staff
Stomp Squad	The SA/ Sturmabteilung/ Brownshirts
Stone	Omaha beach, Normandy

Stoneland	Estonia
Sunflower	Greece
Swarm	Army
Toh	Sicily
Terror Bugs	V-1 flying bombs and V-2 rockets
Treaty of Surrender	Treaty of Versaille
Tweed	Netherlands
U-Bugs	German U-Boats
Underlog	Lidice and Ležáky villages, Czechoslovakia
Venus Jail	Landsberg Prison, Germany
Verge	Spain
Vermen Dungroll	Adolf Hitler, German führer
Vine	Malaysia
Waerozan	Luftwaffe / German Air Force
Water scorpions	Nazi battleships: Bismarck, Tirpitz, Scharnhorst and Gneseinau
WETA	The Gestapo
Willow Waterbase	Pearl Harbor
Wisp	Rotterdam
Wreckz	Blitz

ACKNOWLEDGMENTS

Firstly a huge thank you to Sebastián Valencia for creating a wonderfully illustrated book. Thanks also to Cristian Docolomansky (inks), Macarena Cortes (colours) and Leonardo Venegas (pencils). I must also acknowledge Aliki Paris for all of her careful proofreading work. The staff of the Imperial War Museum and the Holocaust Educational Trust both based in London were particularly helpful. I would also like to acknowledge my grandfather Christopher Okoro, a British Commonwealth soldier of the *not* forgotten Burma campaign. His incredible wartime tales, passed down by my mother to me, stoked my passion for WW2 history and storytelling. Special thanks also to the London Underground upon whose trains this book was written. Finally to my wife and daughters who inspire me to write more.

ABOUT THE AUTHOR

J.D. Okoro is a London-based author of historical fiction, nonfiction articles and some children's stories.
You can follow him on Twitter @JDOkoroAuthor

ABOUT THE ILLUSTRATOR

Sebastián Valencia is a Chilean illustrator, designer and comic book artist based in Buenos Aires, Argentina. Every day he splits himself between drawings, designs and family.
You can follow him on Instagram www.instagram.com/papa_yeah